Stolen Science

**Thirteen Untold Stories of Scientists and
Inventors Almost Written out of History**

Also by Ella Schwartz

Can You Crack the Code?

STOLEN SCIENCE

SCIENCE

Thirteen Untold Stories of Scientists and Inventors Almost Written out of History

ELLA SCHWARTZ

illustrated by
GABY D'ALESSANDRO

BLOOMSBURY
CHILDREN'S BOOKS
NEW YORK LONDON OXFORD NEW DELHI SYDNEY

For Harrison, Sammy, and Nate. Always look for the truth.
—E. S.

For Gail. Thank you for being my mentor and friend.
—G. D.

BLOOMSBURY CHILDREN'S BOOKS
Bloomsbury Publishing Inc., part of Bloomsbury Publishing Plc
1385 Broadway, New York, NY 10018

BLOOMSBURY, BLOOMSBURY CHILDREN'S BOOKS, and the Diana logo
are trademarks of Bloomsbury Publishing Plc

First published in the United States of America in August 2021
by Bloomsbury Children's Books

Text copyright © 2021 by Ella Schwartz
Illustrations copyright © 2021 by Gaby D'Alessandro

Bloomsbury books may be purchased for business or promotional use. For information on bulk purchases please contact
Macmillan Corporate and Premium Sales Department at specialmarkets@macmillan.com

Library of Congress Cataloging-in-Publication Data
available upon request
ISBN 978-1-5476-0228-5 (hardcover) • ISBN 978-1-5476-0229-2 (e-book)

Book design by John Candell
Printed in China by Leo Paper Products, Heshan, Guangdong
2 4 6 8 10 9 7 5 3 1

To find out more about our authors and books visit www.bloomsbury.com and sign up for our newsletters.

TABLE OF CONTENTS

INTRODUCTION

When you think of history's most famous scientists and inventors, who do you think of?

Albert Einstein? Thomas Edison? Galileo Galilei? Charles Darwin? Sure, these were very famous scientists, but history's most important scientists are not all serious-looking gentlemen with fluffy hair or fluffy beards who were classically educated in prominent universities. Certainly these men were scholarly, but not all important scientists and inventors looked like these guys. Where are the women researchers? Where are the Black inventors? Where are the immigrant scientists?

Sometimes history is a big lie.

If I challenged you to name a well-known woman scientist, who would you think of? Maybe you'd say Marie Curie. Sure! Marie Curie was a brilliant scientist. Can you think of anyone else? Jane Goodall might come to mind. Katherine Johnson has recently gained the attention she so deserved. But what took so long?

Why don't we hear stories of more women, people of color, and immigrants in the sciences?

It's most definitely not because these groups weren't performing groundbreaking work. It's because of something else.

Over the centuries, certain scientists and inventors have been overlooked time and again, not because their work wasn't brilliant, but because of who they were. For much of history, discriminated groups including women, people of color, and immigrants often had to claw their way past biases, only to have the credit for their discoveries stolen by their colleagues. It's time to set the record straight and give credit where credit is due.

This book will finally celebrate the achievements of important, often underrepresented, scientists, engineers, and inventors. It will also expose that history isn't always as it may seem.

MARY ANNING

1799-1847

One day, when Mary Anning was just a baby, she was being held by a neighbor, who stood with two other ladies under an elm tree. The group was watching a horse show pass by when, suddenly, lightning struck the tree, instantly killing all three ladies. Baby Mary was in critical condition. She was rushed home and revived in a tub of hot water. The village doctor declared the baby's survival a miracle. This may have been the first remarkable experience of young Mary's life, but it would not be the last.

The Anning family lived in the town of Lyme Regis, England, at the turn of the nineteenth century. Mary's dad was a carpenter, but his wages were barely enough to feed his family. To supplement his income, he would often sell sea trinkets to tourists. These souvenirs, sometimes called curios by the locals, had names like snake stones and devil's fingers. Some tourists believed these curios had magical powers.

Were these curios actually magical? Did they have mystical properties? Were they otherworldly? These curios were, indeed, from an unrecognizable world long forgotten. But they were not magical. They were actually bone fragments of ancient creatures: fossils.

Back in the early 1800s, fossil hunting, or paleontology, wasn't a science like it is today. It was more of a hobby. The town of Lyme Regis, England, now known as the Jurassic Coast, had plenty of fossils if you knew where and how to look for them. The town bordered the ocean, and after big rainstorms, some of the rock cliffs would break away and fall into the sea, exposing evidence of an ancient world below. Since the money from fossil selling was so important to the Anning family, Dad often took Mary and her brother Joseph along on fossil-hunting outings. He trained them to spot fossils in the cliffs of Lyme Regis and to carefully remove these ancient treasures from the limestone.

But fossil hunting in the cliffs of Lyme Regis was a dangerous business. The Anning family had to wade through the water around unstable cliffs, looking for specimens that may have fallen from the recent rockfall. Rockfalls often led to more rockfalls and mudslides, usually without any warning. Sadly, Mary's dad was seriously injured in an accident while searching the unstable cliffs of Lyme Regis and later died from complications of these injuries.

The Anning family was left with practically nothing. To survive, Mary and Joseph, just young kids themselves, had no choice but to continue their father's fossil-hunting work and hope for some good finds. If they peddled curios to visiting tourists, they might earn enough money for food.

Luckily their father taught them well.

Young Mary and Joseph ventured out to the cliffs, now all alone, in search of ancient treasures. Most of the time their hauls would be seashells or small fragments. These finds were barely enough to feed the struggling Anning family. And then, in 1811, Joseph spotted something they had never seen in the rock wall. After excavating the specimen, Joseph and Mary realized they had something that was far more unusual than seashells. This was a four-foot-long skull of some kind of sea creature.

Joseph, as the oldest Anning child, had no choice but to take on responsibilities to support the family. When he stumbled upon the discovery of the ancient sea creature's skull, he was already working as an apprentice. This was an important opportunity for Joseph and would earn him steady wages to help support his widowed mother and young sister. Joseph didn't have much time for fossil hunting anymore.

But Mary was excited by the skull her brother had found and had a suspicion there may be more bones nearby. Surely a head must go together with other body parts? Mary returned to the site, determined to find more of the sea creature. She made a crucial discovery that would change her life forever. Sure enough, in the area near where the skull had been found, she spotted more bones. Mary deduced these bones must belong to the same creature whose skull they had already unearthed. She was so excited by her discovery, she recruited an excavation team to help her remove the bones from the rocks. It took the team many months, but when their work was complete, and they reunited all the bones with the skull, they had the complete skeleton of an astonishing seventeen-foot-long sea creature.

People in the village of Lyme Regis thought Mary had uncovered a monster. A creature with the form of the skeleton discovered by Mary had never been seen before. It looked like a cross between a dolphin and a crocodile. Most people at the time assumed that this fish-lizard creature had migrated away from Lyme Regis to some faraway land. The villagers were probably grateful that this monster was no longer lurking nearby. The idea that this animal was actually extinct would probably not have occurred to them as extinction was a science that was not yet accepted.

It turned out the remains discovered by Mary belonged to a dinosaur called ichthyosaur. Mary's dinosaur was not the first ichthyosaur discovered, but it was the most complete skeleton of its time. News about Mary's dinosaur began to spread, attracting interest from Great Britain's scientists and collectors. Mary sold the fossil to the lord of a nearby manor, and it eventually found its way to a museum in Great Britain. In return, Mary received enough money to feed the Anning family for six months.

Mary had just made one of the most important fossil discoveries of her time and had earned enough money to support her family. Not too bad for a girl who wasn't even thirteen years old yet!

The ichthyosaur was the first of Mary's many important scientific discoveries, but she didn't get any credit for this groundbreaking work. Her discovery was used in one of the very first scientific papers ever written about the ichthyosaur, published in 1814 by Everard Home, who is considered a founder of paleontology. In fact, many scientific papers followed the Home paper, and none of them ever credited Mary with the discovery of the fossils. Mary was but a poor, uneducated girl. The esteemed gentlemen of science and power of Great Britain felt that the generous payment made to Mary was more than enough to reward her discovery. Meanwhile, these same gentlemen were earning fame and fortune as a result of Mary's work.

Mary carried on, combing the shores of Lyme Regis for more ancient fossils, but as she got older, she decided to learn more about the science behind her work. She studied scientific papers and scientific methods, which were challenging for a young girl with a very limited education to understand. She mastered different techniques used by museums for preparing and preserving fossils. She practiced drawing specimens and became an expert at scientific illustrations. She learned the anatomy of all sorts of animals and was able to compare the structure of her fossil finds to those of living creatures. This helped her explain how prehistoric creatures lived and helped her guess how they may have become extinct.

She even taught herself French so she could read and understand the works of an important French paleontologist, a man named Georges Cuvier. Cuvier was a legendary scientist in those days, but published his research in French, which, of course, Mary didn't understand.

While Mary was becoming an expert paleontologist, most people in Britain rejected the evidence emerging from her science: that extinction was real. The common belief was that Earth was only a few thousand years old and animals could never disappear from existence. These never-before-seen creatures that Mary and other paleontologists of her time were digging up challenged these ideas. Fossils suggested an ancient world existed millions of years before humans. This idea went against everything people were taught to believe, especially the teachings of the church. Charles Darwin's groundbreaking theory of evolution would not be published until forty years in the future. To explain away these mysterious fossils, some people declared these vanished creatures weren't extinct, but had simply relocated.

In 1823, when Mary Anning was only twenty-four years old, she would make another incredible discovery. While on a fossil-hunting mission, she came upon a fossil skull that looked different from anything she had seen before. Over her years of searching for fossils in Lyme Regis, most of the skulls she found belonged to the ichthyosaur. She knew that this new, bizarre-looking skull was definitely not that of the ichthyosaur. She went on to dig up the rest of the animal's body. The full skeleton was nine feet long and was the strangest creature Mary had ever seen.

Mary knew that some of the most famous paleontologists at the time suspected that bones previously believed to belong to the ichthyosaur actually belonged to a completely different sea creature called the plesiosaur. Mary had a suspicion that this bizarre skeleton she had just discovered may be that very creature. She contacted paleontologists she trusted in Europe, sending detailed illustrations of the sea creature and sharing her suspicions.

But not everyone believed Mary's theory. One of the most vocal challengers of Mary's plesiosaur discovery was the same Georges Cuvier whose works had inspired Mary to learn French. Cuvier announced that Mary's discovery was a fake. He claimed the proportions of the fossil, with a tiny head and a very long neck, could not be possible, and pronounced Mary's entire discovery a big hoax. This was a major blow to Mary. She had made a truly amazing discovery of her own and this man mocked her. If Cuvier could convince other scientists that Mary was a fraud, her reputation would be ruined forever.

A special meeting was called at the Geological Society of London to discuss and review Mary's plesiosaur discovery. All the most important paleontologists of the time were invited, including Georges Cuvier. Mary was not permitted to attend. Women were not welcome at such scientific events. During this meeting, Mary's fossils were closely examined and debated. Eventually, the scientists all agreed that Mary's plesiosaur fossils were, indeed, real. Even Cuvier, who had the chance to closely inspect the bones of this new creature, admitted Mary's discovery was not only genuine, but also one of the most amazing fossil discoveries ever made.

Mary Anning went on to make many other important discoveries. For example, she began the study of coprolites, which are fossilized poop. But Mary was not widely credited for pioneering the study of coprolites or dozens of important dinosaur fossil finds. Other scientists published her discoveries and profited from her research. Mary's name was never mentioned in

MARY BEGAN THE STUDY OF COPROLITES, WHICH ARE FOSSILIZED POOP.

any scientific publications. She couldn't publish her own research because reputable science journals would not accept submissions from women. Mary often lamented that the world was unfair and unkind to her.

When Mary was in her forties, she became sick with cancer. By then, the Geological Society of London still hadn't accepted Mary as a scientist, but they did appreciate her contribution as a fossil collector. She had helped make a lot of male scientists in the society very successful with her fossil finds. But while many of the society's members had become rich and famous, Mary was still living a poor life. The society, acknowledging her contribution, started a fund to help pay for Mary's cancer treatments, but Mary died of cancer at the age of forty-seven.

In life, Mary was never accepted as a member of the Geological Society of London. Today, the society has one of Mary's ichthyosaur skulls and a portrait of her in their reception hall.

The Jurassic Coast where Mary Anning first shaped the science of paleontology and raised questions about the history of Earth was named a UNESCO World Heritage Site in 2001. To earn this honor, a landmark must be judged by the United Nations to be historically important because of remarkable accomplishments made there. Today, Mary's legacy lives on, as the next generation of fossil hunters look for new discoveries in the cliffs of Lyme Regis.

What's the SCIENCE?

PALEONTOLOGY IS THE BRANCH of science that helps us understand what life on Earth may have looked like millions of years ago, well before the existence of humans. Paleontologists use fossils to help them draw their conclusions. When people think of fossils, they might imagine dinosaur bones. This isn't entirely complete. Fossils can form not just from dinosaur remains, but also from any animal and even plants. What all fossils do have in common is they all provide evidence of life lived a long time ago.

There are all different types of fossils paleontologists look for. Some fossils aren't formed from an animal itself, but from an animal's activities. An example of this might be a footprint that an animal made in mud that, over time, hardened and became preserved. The footprint might provide valuable information to a scientist, such as how big the animal was and how it might have moved.

Other types of fossils that paleontologists hunt resemble bones. Most people are familiar with the image of an enormous skeletal dinosaur in a museum. You may be surprised to learn that those bones aren't actually bones. They are rocks!

12

How are dinosaur fossils formed?

Not all dinosaurs that roamed the earth became fossilized. The conditions had to be just right for fossils to form. When the dinosaur died, it would have to have been buried very quickly by mud, sand, or dirt. This is called sediment. Over time, more and more sediment would have to cover the dinosaur's remains. As the sediment layer grew thicker and thicker, it would eventually harden into rock. Beneath the rock, the dinosaur remains would decay, and small spaces would form within the bones. Those spaces would fill up with new minerals from groundwater spreading through the sediment. Eventually the entire bone would be replaced by these new minerals. The resulting fossil is made of completely different materials from the original organism, but the mineral deposits take its exact same shape.

JO ANDERSON

If you were an American farmer in the early 1800s, your work wasn't easy. At harvest time, you would toil from morning until night in the hot fields. You would use tools like scythes and sickles to cut the grain stalks, swinging the heavy tools over and over until the harvest was complete. It would take one person an entire day to harvest just two acres of wheat. By the end of the day, you would be drenched in sweat, your muscles sore.

That is, until Cyrus McCormick invented the mechanical reaper—a wheat-cutting machine. With the reaper, instead of spending the whole day performing backbreaking work to harvest just two acres of wheat, a farmer could cut up to ten acres, with practically no effort. And in the 1800s, this was a really big deal. Before the reaper, big farms were simply too hard for one farmer and his family to manage. On a big farm, it would have been impossible to cut and bundle all the grain before the crops would, eventually, rot and spoil. The problem was, because the harvesting process took so long and involved so much physical labor, most families during the fall growing season couldn't cut enough grain to last them until the next harvest. Back then, you couldn't just walk into a supermarket to buy grain. Farmers relied on their own crops to feed their families through the long winter months.

It is said that Cyrus McCormick's invention of the mechanical reaper was one of the most important inventions of his time, transforming the country. Since farm labor wasn't as difficult as it had been, farmers could plant more crops, which meant families didn't have to be scared about having enough to feed their families. Not only was there plenty of grain to sustain a family through the winter, but also the grain was so plentiful that farmers could now export it to other states and even across the ocean to Europe, which brought in a lot of money. The economy was now booming.

And since farmwork was less difficult, every member of a family wasn't forced to be a farmer. People were now free to pursue other jobs, like working in schools, factories, or banks. This was a great opportunity for the American workforce and sparked the American Industrial Revolution.

The mechanical reaper was, without question, a very important invention.

Many historical reports claim that it took Cyrus McCormick just six weeks to perfect his design for the mechanical reaper. Once his magnificent invention was ready, Cyrus decided it was time to demonstrate the reaper in action. He welcomed friends, neighbors, and nearby farmers to a small field near Steeles Tavern, Virginia. There, the spectators watched and cheered as a horse rode through the fields, pulling the mechanical reaper along as it cut a wide path through the grainfields in no time. Cyrus McCormick walked proudly behind his invention. He knew the reaper was about to change the world.

And he wasn't wrong. The reaper did change the world.

Except, claims that Cyrus McCormick completed the design and proto-type for the reaper in six weeks is, without a doubt, stretching the truth—in more ways than one.

The truth is, Cyrus McCormick wasn't the only mastermind behind the mechanical reaper. Cyrus's dad, Robert McCormick, worked on a design for the mechanical reaper for over twenty years at the McCormick family's Wal-nut Grove plantation. As a young boy, Cyrus worked alongside his father to craft and perfect the plans for the mechanical reaper. It's safe to say, Cyrus merely improved upon his father's ingenuity.

But, that's not the entire story. It turns out, Cyrus McCormick could never have completed a successful design for the mechanical reaper if it weren't for a man named Jo Anderson.

Jo Anderson was present that day in Steeles Tavern, during the first public demonstration of the mechanical reaper. He walked behind the horse-led reaper, raking the sheared grain stalks from the reaper's plat-form. Friends and neighbors in attendance that day in Steeles Tavern likely assumed Jo Anderson was just following McCormick's orders. They had no idea that Jo Anderson was one of the masterminds behind an invention that was about to revolutionize America.

Jo Anderson was born at the McCormick family's Walnut Grove

plantation in 1808. Cyrus McCormick was born a year later. The two boys grew up together at Walnut Grove, one an enslaved Black child, one a free white child.

Jo spent a lot of time in the fields cutting and bundling wheat stalks, so Jo knew a lot about cutting wheat. While Jo worked the fields, Cyrus learned to read and write. As Cyrus got older and started tinkering with his father's design for the reaper, he needed help from someone who knew a thing or two about cutting wheat. By then, Jo Anderson was an expert. Jo began working with Cyrus to create different prototype designs for the mechanical reaper. He worked alongside him for months tweaking the design, working as a blacksmith to forge parts, and assembling the components for the mechanical reaper.

After successfully demonstrating the workings of the mechanical reaper at Steeles Tavern, Cyrus McCormick applied for a patent for the invention with the US government. A patent gives an inventor ownership of the invention and stops other people from making or using their invention without permission. Cyrus McCormick was granted a patent for the mechanical reaper in 1834. This patent proclaimed that Cyrus was the inventor of the reaper.

PATENT RULES AT THAT TIME DID NOT ALLOW **ENSLAVED PEOPLE** TO BE CREDITED WITH PATENTS.

Cyrus didn't give credit to Jo in his patent application. Patent rules at that time did not allow enslaved people to be credited with patents. If Cyrus wanted the US government to grant him a patent for the mechanical reaper, he would need to keep Jo Anderson's role in the invention a secret.

In 1847 Cyrus, together with his brother, started the McCormick Harvesting Company. They built a huge factory in Chicago to manufacture and sell reapers. Cyrus and his family became very wealthy. Cyrus did release

Jo from enslavement shortly before the Civil War, but Jo never received the same wealth and fame as that of his co-inventor. Later, Cyrus encouraged Jo to join him in Chicago, but Jo decided it was best for his family to remain in Virginia. Cyrus purchased a log cabin for Jo. It is true that Cyrus often sent money, food, and clothing to help support Jo, but Jo lived a very modest life. The money sent by Cyrus was never used for anything fancy. It was only used for Jo and his family's basic needs.

The McCormick Harvesting Company later became the International Harvester Company. In 1931, when the company celebrated the one-hundred-year anniversary of the invention of the reaper, a special medallion was made. On one side of the medallion was an image of none other than Jo Anderson walking beside the horse-drawn reaper. The medallion served to publicly honor Jo Anderson's role in the invention.

Cyrus McCormick was an exceptional businessman. By promoting the mechanical reaper, he transformed America forever. But the businessman wouldn't have had an invention to sell had it not been for Jo Anderson.

BEFORE THE INVENTION OF the mechanical reaper to assist in harvesting crops, there was the reaper. A reaper was a person who "reaped" crops by hand. This person would need to cut the crops, usually with a hand tool. The crops would fall to the ground. After the reaper cleared a plot of land, they would need to go back and collect the stalks and gather them into bunches for storing.

The mechanical reaper helped make the job of harvesting much simpler. The hard part of the work was all but eliminated. Instead of a person having to swing a cutting tool to chop at each individual stalk of grain, a horse-drawn machine would do most of the heavy work. As the horses moved across the grainfield, a bunch of stalks were gathered and held. At the same time, a spinning knife chopped away at the collected stalks. The cut stalks were then pushed back onto a platform. This happened in a continuous motion as the horses slowly pulled the contraption through the field. The only energy needed would be that required by the horses as they slowly walked through the field while towing the reaping machine behind them.

When the grain filled the platform, it would be raked to the ground in a big pile. It could then be easily bundled and tied. This eliminated the need to gather the stalks wherever they dropped in the field.

ANTONIO MEUCCI

1808-1889

L et's admit it. We're all guilty of taking the telephone for granted. Today we rely on our phones to instantly communicate with friends and family. Imagine how different life would be without telephones. Think about how annoying it would be not to be able to instantly share important news with friends and family. How frustrating would everyday life be if your only method of communication was writing letters and sending them by mail? And yet, before the late 1870s and the invention of the telephone, this was exactly how most people communicated.

When the telephone was invented, this device seemed almost too good to be true. Imagine! If someone wanted to communicate important news, they no longer had to write a letter and wait days or weeks for the news to arrive by mail. Suddenly, all they'd have to do was pick up a receiver, and they could talk in real time to anybody they wanted, anywhere in the world.

On March 7, 1876, Alexander Graham Bell was awarded a patent for the telephone. To be awarded a patent, an inventor or scientist must prove that their invention or discovery is original. This is as true today as it was back then. A patent announces to the world that the invention is the property of the inventor and nobody else. The same way it is illegal to steal someone's stuff, it is illegal to steal someone's invention idea when they hold a patent.

Except here's the funny thing about a patent: it's just a piece of paper. On the day that Bell was awarded the patent, he had never actually managed to get a telephone to work. The patent described a great idea, but could it really be possible?

Once Bell was granted the patent, he immediately set off in his Boston, Massachusetts, laboratory, alongside his assistant, Thomas Watson, to build a functioning telephone. It only took him three days, but Bell finally had something he thought might actually work. To test his device, Bell set up a telephone in his room on the top floor of his house and ran wires to a receiving telephone one floor below. Then Bell spoke the following words into the telephone: "Mr. Watson, come here. I want you."

Seconds later, Watson burst into Bell's room, exclaiming, "I heard you. I could hear what you said." He had heard Bell's voice clearly, even though he was in another room of the house with walls separating them.

At the time, those first spoken words were an incredible technological breakthrough. And yet, it's one thing to transmit a human voice across a short distance, only a few rooms away, but could the telephone actually transmit speech across an entire neighborhood? Across the country? How about across an ocean?

Thirty-eight years later, that question was finally answered when Bell and his assistant, Watson, talked by telephone to each other across a distance of 3,400 miles. Bell was in New York, and Watson was on the other side of the country, in California. There were huge audiences in attendance on both ends of the country, including the president of the United States, Woodrow Wilson. Bell said, "Mr. Watson, are you there?" Watson replied that he was there and could hear Bell perfectly. And then Bell repeated his famous words, the first sentence ever spoken through a telephone: "Mr. Watson, come here. I want you."

Mr. Watson replied, "It would take me a week to get to you this time."

The crowd erupted in thunderous applause. The telephone was a huge success.

From then, the telephone became an integral part of our everyday lives, forever changing the way people communicate and interact across the world.

Surely, we owe a debt of gratitude to Alexander Graham Bell for shaping our world.

Except, Bell was not the first person to invent the telephone.

The first telephone was actually made by an Italian immigrant by the name of Antonio Meucci. In fact, Antonio Meucci was using a working telephone *he* invented decades before Bell had even applied for a patent.

Antonio Meucci was born in Florence, Italy. When he was only thirteen years old, he was admitted to the Academy of Fine Arts, where he studied subjects like physics and engineering. After finishing his studies, he took a job at a Florence theater house where he put his knowledge to good use, working as a theater stage technician. He began showing his inventive side when he built a working communication system between the stage and the control room. It was at this job that he met his wife, Ester.

Upon leaving Florence, Meucci first moved to Cuba, where he developed a way to treat illnesses with electric shocks. This may sound barbaric, but in the 1830s, this was a very popular medical treatment. One day, while preparing to administer an electric shock treatment to a friend suffering from migraines,

HE REALIZED THAT SOUND, AND THUS HUMAN VOICE, COULD TRAVEL BY **ELECTRICITY THROUGH WIRE**.

Meucci made a startling discovery. He was able to hear his friend's voice, who was in another room, across a copper wire running between them. He realized that sound, and thus human voice, could travel by electricity through wire. Meucci sensed he was on to something major. This spark of ingenuity was the early design of the telephone.

The year was 1849. And Alexander Graham Bell was only two years old.

In 1850, Meucci moved from Cuba to Staten Island, New York, to continue his research and develop the technology for the telephone. But he quickly discovered the challenges of being an immigrant. Back in Cuba, he could rely on the similarities between the Spanish and Italian languages to get by, but here in America, communicating in English was nearly impossible. He was also discriminated against because of his nationality. Back then, Italians were often the subject of cruel bigotry. They were not treated fairly in business, and were not even permitted to hold management positions at most jobsites. This made business dealings very challenging.

But that didn't stop him from continuing his efforts.

Sadly, a few years later, Antonio Meucci's wife became ill, then paralyzed. Wanting to make sure Ester was okay while he worked in his lab, Meucci rigged a system that allowed him to speak with her from her bedroom while he was in his workshop. He called his invention the *telettrofono*. The year was

1856. This was more than twenty years before Bell allegedly spoke those famous words across the wire to his assistant, Watson.

But now Meucci faced a new challenge: how would an immigrant who couldn't speak English and who had very little money promote his magnificent new invention?

Meucci figured if anyone would be willing to help him, it would be his own countrymen. He begged rich Italian families for assistance but didn't get very far. Meucci even published his invention in a New York Italian-language newspaper, hoping to gain some interest, but that didn't help either. Soon, Antonio Meucci was bankrupt. His house was eventually seized and auctioned. The purchaser was kind enough to let the Meuccis stay in the house without paying rent, but with no money, Meucci was forced to live off the generosity of his friends and small distributions of money the government gave poor families to help cover basic living expenses.

Crushed but not beaten, Meucci continued working hard to improve his design for the telephone. He had come to America because it was the land of opportunity. He believed in the potential of his invention. If he could perfect the design and find the right financial backers, all of the hardship would be worth it.

But then tragedy struck.

One day, while traveling home from Manhattan, the ferryboat Meucci was riding exploded. Meucci was rushed to the hospital with severe burns. He stayed in the hospital for months recovering from the accident. His wife was forced to sell all of his telettrofono models and designs to a pawnshop for six dollars to help pay for his medical expenses.

Eventually, Meucci recovered and was released from the hospital, but without his telephone models, his dreams of becoming a famous inventor were almost destroyed. He tried to recover his models, but the pawnshop had already sold them. His telettrofono models were gone. But instead of wallowing in self-pity, Meucci worked day and night to reconstruct his models. And in the process, not only did he rebuild his models, but he *perfected* them as well.

Meucci was so confident in his new design for the telephone that he was ready to file for a patent. But there was one problem. He did not have $250 for the patent-filing fees. Instead, he spent ten dollars to file notice of an *impending* patent. This impending patent announced that, while he wasn't prepared to file a full patent, he was getting ready to file a patent. It also protected his invention and ensured nobody could claim a similar invention as their own. The following year, when the impending patent expired, Meucci still wasn't able to file for a full patent, so he paid ten dollars to renew the intent to file. He renewed the impending patent for ten dollars for three years, in 1871, 1872, and 1873. During this time, Meucci was trying really hard to secure funding for his invention and to allow him to file for a full patent. He went to the Western Union Company to see if they would be interested in helping him with his invention. He left the company a working prototype of his telephone along with the paperwork for his patent intentions. Years passed, but Western Union never contacted Meucci again. After repeatedly asking Western Union to return his prototype and documentation, the company finally told him they were all lost. For some reason, Meucci failed to file the intent for a patent starting in 1874.

This would be one of the biggest slipups of Antonio Meucci's life.

In 1876, Alexander Graham Bell was awarded a patent for the telephone and became a very rich and very famous man.

Antonio Meucci, who had toiled so hard, who could barely understand English, who had suffered prejudice, and who could not even afford to pay his rent, was left with . . . nothing.

It was also a fact that Alexander Graham Bell conducted experiments in the same Western Union laboratory where Meucci's materials had been left, and supposedly lost. While there is no proof that Bell stole Meucci's prototypes while working at Western Union, it is certainly an odd coincidence.

Meucci would not give up. He knew he had to fight for justice. He had worked too hard.

He decided to take Alexander Graham Bell and his company to court to reclaim what he felt was rightfully his: the patent for the telephone.

After years of back-and-forth legal squabbling, the case finally made it to court in 1886. But by then, Bell was a rich and famous man, with a huge company behind him. Meucci was still a poor Italian immigrant.

Did he really stand a chance?

The Secretary of State at the time thought so. He made a public statement saying that "there exists sufficient proof to give priority to Meucci in the invention of the telephone."

The Secretary of State was an important man. Surely if he thought Meucci should be awarded with the patent, it was a safe bet the judges in the courts would agree, right?

Except several legal cases continued to go back and forth for many years. Antonio Meucci died penniless, without his coveted patent, in 1889. His case was dropped after that, too.

Alexander Graham Bell would go down in history as the inventor of the telephone.

Despite it taking over a hundred years to set the record straight, Antonio Meucci finally got some of the credit he deserved.

In 2002, Staten Island congressman Vito Fossella of the US House of Representatives introduced a resolution stating "that the life and achievements of Antonio Meucci should be recognized, and his work in the invention of the telephone should be acknowledged." The resolution also claimed that if Meucci had been able to pay the ten-dollar fee to maintain his intent to file a patent in 1874, no patent could have been issued to Bell. And while this resolution provided no compensation, nor reversed the awards bestowed on Bell, it finally acknowledged Antonio Meucci's accomplishments.

It took more than one hundred years, but the US government recognized that the true inventor of the telephone was Antonio Meucci.

What's the SCIENCE?

YOU PROBABLY USE A telephone every day, but how does a telephone actually work?

The first thing to understand are the parts of the phone. The top of the phone, which is also the part you press up against your ear, is called the earpiece. The earpiece is really just a speaker. It works just like a speaker you might use to listen to the radio. Its job is to produce sound. The bottom of the phone, near your mouth, is called the mouthpiece. The mouthpiece contains a microphone to help capture your voice.

When you speak into the telephone's mouthpiece, the sound energy of your voice makes the air vibrate. The vibrating air carries the sound energy into the phone. Inside the telephone's mouthpiece is a part called the diaphragm, which converts sound energy into electrical energy.

This electrical energy then travels from your phone to your friend's phone. Once the electrical energy reaches your friend's phone, a diaphragm in the phone's earpiece speaker converts the incoming electrical energy back to sound energy.

This sound energy travels out of the speaker and into your friend's ear. You're now having a phone conversation!

The process described above is the same whether the caller is using a landline, which is a phone that works only in one place, like a house or a business, or a cell phone, which you can take with you anywhere. The main difference between a landline and a cell phone is the way they make calls. A landline uses wires and cables to connect it to other telephones. Cell phones, on the other hand, use radio waves to transmit the calls—no wires needed!

BENJAMIN BRADLEY

ca. 1830–1897

Enslaved people in America in the 1800s had a brutal life. They were often forced to work under harsh conditions, with little rest or comfort. They were not allowed to own property, enter into contracts, or defend themselves against unfair treatment and cruelty. One thing that was definitely not allowed for enslaved people in the 1830s was an education. It was considered illegal for them to learn how to read and write. Those who supported slavery worried that if Blacks were allowed an education, it would help them rally together and revolt. Preventing enslaved people from learning was a way of ensuring they would continue to live in bondage.

But that didn't stop Benjamin Bradley.

Benjamin Bradley was born sometime in the 1830s. His exact date of birth is unknown because births and deaths of enslaved people in that time were not often officially recorded. What is known is that he was born into slavery and lived with a family in Annapolis, Maryland. Some believe that Bradley learned how to read and write from his enslaver's children. This set the course of Bradley's path to success and freedom.

While enslaved people in the South mainly worked the fields on large plantations, in the North, agriculture was not as big of an industry. Benjamin Bradley was sent to work in a printing office. There, he analyzed how different machines worked. He tinkered with the devices, studying how the parts operated together. As a young teenager with a spark of imagination, Bradley would collect scraps from around the shop and use them as parts to build new contraptions. From junk he collected, like a gun barrel, some pewter, and pieces of round steel, Bradley was able to design and build a working model for a steam engine. This was a remarkable achievement for an enslaved teenager with no formal schooling.

Bradley's enslavers recognized that he was smart, hardworking, and capable. They were able to get him a job as a helper at the US Naval Academy. There he continued to work hard, impress his bosses, and learn as much as he could. Bradley was paid for his work, but because he was an enslaved person, as was customary at the time, the money he earned had to go to his enslavers.

The enslaver, however, allowed Bradley to keep five dollars a month out of his wages for himself. Today, that would be about $130. That's hardly enough to live on for an entire month, but it was something.

While working at the Naval Academy, Bradley realized he was sitting on an opportunity. The Naval Academy was filled with sailors. And sailors like ships. He decided to sell the model he built from scrap junk to a student at the academy. He took this money, combined it with the meager savings he was permitted to keep from his wages, and designed and built his most impressive invention: the first steam engine strong enough to power a warship at a rate of sixteen knots an hour. This is a speed of about eighteen miles per hour. It wasn't the first steam engine ever invented, but it was the first steam engine that provided such remarkable horsepower for its time. Warships today travel at speeds much faster than this, but back then, a speedy steam-powered sloop of war was a game changer.

> IT WAS THE FIRST STEAM ENGINE THAT PROVIDED **SUCH REMARKABLE HORSEPOWER** FOR ITS TIME.

Bradley was sitting on an invention that could change America's military dominance forever. Such a noteworthy invention was deserving of awards, praises, and honors. But there was one big problem that made it impossible for Benjamin Bradley to get the credit he rightfully deserved. A patent would announce to everyone that Bradley was the mastermind behind the ship's steam engine. It would guarantee that nobody could steal or use his invention without permission. But in America in the 1800s, a patent for an enslaved Black man was prohibited.

With no possibility of securing a patent for his hard work, Bradley knew his options were limited. Without a patent, he couldn't promote and profit from his invention. But such an important engineering breakthrough deserved more than being tucked away and ignored. Bradley made a choice that would not only change the course of naval engineering but would also change the course of his own life.

Bradley was able to sell the designs for the engine and keep the money for himself. He lost the rights to his invention, but with the money earned from selling the engine, combined with the money he had saved from his employment, he was able to buy his freedom.

Benjamin Bradley lived the rest of his life a free man.

What's the SCIENCE?

IT TAKES ENERGY TO walk, to ride a bike, to power a car, and to fly an airplane. An engine is a machine that converts energy into motion. A steam engine runs using two essential ingredients: fire and water.

Imagine a kettle on a stove. The fire from the stove heats the water inside the kettle. When the water is hot enough, it boils, creating steam. Now imagine if you could harness the energy of the steam jetting out of the kettle to power a machine. That is exactly how a steam engine works.

In a steam engine, heat energy is produced by burning coal. The coal gets extremely hot, which in turn heats water stored in a big tank. When the water in the tank is heated to a high enough temperature, it begins to boil, producing steam. The thrust of the steam gushing out of the tank drives a piston back and forth. The movement of the piston can then be used as energy to turn a wheel or power a machine.

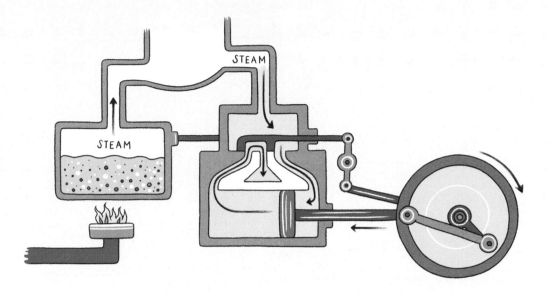

The invention of the steam engine transformed transportation and sparked America's Industrial Revolution. Steam engines were widely used in trains to carry people and cargo great distances across the country. Eventually, steam engines became an important power source for water transportation. These steam-powered ships no longer needed to rely on wind-powered sails for movement. Instead, a steam engine produced enough energy to power a spinning paddlewheel that gave the ship movement.

CARLOS JUAN FINLAY

1833–1915

Although Cuba is now an independent country, it took many years and lots of fighting before it won its independence from Spain in 1898. In later years, Cuba and America would develop a strained relationship, but in the late 1800s, just a few short years after the US Civil War, America had a keen interest in helping Cuba. Cuba's proximity to the United States—just a few hundred miles off the coast of Florida—made it an extremely strategic location. To be sure, the United States was not thrilled with the Spanish Empire's being so close to their own shores.

Cuban revolutionaries had been fighting the Spanish for independence for many years. The United States kept close watch on the situation, but despite a lot of Americans supporting a war to help the Cubans gain their independence, the American government decided to hang back, monitor the situation, and help from afar.

That all changed in January 1898, when President William McKinley sent the US battleship USS *Maine* to the shores of Cuba to help protect American interests in the region. Shortly after the *Maine*'s arrival in Havana Harbor, on February 15, the battleship was destroyed by a massive explosion. The ship was blown to pieces, killing 260 people on board. Although nobody knew for sure who was responsible for the explosion, many people blamed Spain.

President McKinley resisted going to war, but after the *Maine*'s destruction, public pressure to help the Cubans and seek revenge for the destroyed battleship became too great. In April, the United States declared war with Spain, and just two months later, American soldiers entered Cuba. After a few short weeks, the war was over.

The soldiers didn't know it at the time, but they were fighting a more lethal enemy than the Spanish. This enemy was a disease. About four hundred American lives were lost during the war as a result of combat. But nearly two thousand lives would be lost to a disease known as yellow fever.

Even after the war was over, American troops stayed in Cuba to help the Cubans establish an independent country and protect American interests in the region. Theodore Roosevelt, who would later become president of the United States, led a group of soldiers in the region and begged his superiors to allow the soldiers to leave before they became infected with the deadly disease. He wrote, "If we are kept here it will in all human possibility mean an appalling disaster, for the surgeons here estimate that over half the army, if kept here during the sickly season, will die."

Theodore Roosevelt was a smart man. He knew yellow fever was no joke. It had devastated the US Army much more than the Spanish forces had. The United States now had no choice. If Cuba was to become a strategic stronghold, they had to find a way to stop yellow fever.

Shortly after the war, a special medical commission was formed to study yellow fever. The commission was led by a man named Walter Reed. The goal of this commission was to figure out how yellow fever spread from person to person. Walter Reed reasoned that if they could figure out how the disease spread, they could find a way to stop it. Reed and his team traveled to Cuba to study the disease firsthand.

Reed's team began their work by evaluating the most popular yellow fever theories of the time. Some people believed that yellow fever was transmitted through contaminated objects. The idea behind this theory went something like this: a person infected with yellow fever would cover themselves with a blanket. Later, if a noninfected person used that same blanket, they would get the disease. Walter Reed and his commission quickly realized that this theory, and many other common beliefs, were plain wrong.

There was one man, however, who had figured out the mysteries of yellow fever twenty years before Walter Reed stepped foot inside Cuba.

Carlos Juan Finlay was a Cuban who had earned his medical degree in the United States. He was encouraged by his medical school colleagues to begin his career in America, but his love for his native country pulled him back to Cuba. There, he earned a reputation for being a kind and compassionate doctor. He never turned away a patient who was unable to pay for medical services.

In 1879, nearly twenty years before the start of the Spanish American War, Finlay was asked by the Cuban government to study yellow fever. The disease was crippling the island. Families were terrified of getting sick. Finlay got to work to try to understand more about the disease and how it might spread.

Two years later Finlay believed he had his answer. He presented his findings at a conference in Washington, DC. His hypothesis was that mosquitoes were responsible for the transmission of yellow fever. His theory was mostly ignored. Nobody believed that a mosquito could spread the virus.

Finlay was not discouraged. He continued to perform experiments to test his theory. One of his experiments involved having a mosquito bite a person infected with yellow fever, then having that same mosquito go on to bite a healthy person. In some cases, but not all of them, the healthy person would go on to develop yellow fever. In other cases, it seemed the person would develop an immunity to yellow fever. These results were curious, but seemed to prove that a mosquito was indeed responsible for transmitting the disease.

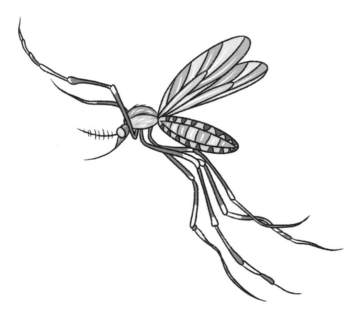

The problem was, many people took Finlay's varying results as proof that the mosquito couldn't possibly be responsible for spreading the disease. If the mosquito was the reason behind the spread of yellow fever, then surely all of Finlay's test subjects bitten by an exposed mosquito would contract the disease. Finlay became a laughingstock in medical circles. Some people even called him the "crazy Cuban doctor."

Finlay pressed on and never wavered in his belief that the mosquito was to blame for the spread of yellow fever. He knew he could prove his theories with further experimentation, like if he allowed his test subjects to receive multiple bites from contaminated mosquitoes or by letting the mosquitoes have a longer incubation period before biting the test subjects. However, if he conducted these further experiments, his test subjects could get extremely sick, and maybe even die. He refused to attempt those experiments on his test subjects. Those people had put their trust in the Cuban doctor. Finlay did not want to abuse that trust. His purpose in human experimentation was to identify the method of transmission, and he believed that he had proved, without a shadow of a doubt, that the answer was mosquitoes. There was no reason to put humans at risk just to satisfy his critics.

For twenty years, he continued to research and study mosquitoes as the reason behind the spread of yellow fever, amassing an enormous amount of research data. When Walter Reed and his team arrived in Cuba, Finlay quickly sought them out in the hopes of sharing his findings. Fresh out of ideas, Walter Reed had no choice but to listen.

Initially, Reed did not believe the mosquito theory. The idea was so different from everything else that had been proposed, it hardly seemed possible. His colleagues didn't much believe the mosquito theory either. Two of them even allowed themselves to be bitten by Finlay's contaminated mosquitoes. A few days later, they both became sick with yellow fever. One eventually recovered, but the other died.

It seemed clear to Walter Reed at that point that Finlay's mosquito theory was worth a closer look. He performed experiments to determine if other factors might be contributing to the spread of the disease. Eventually, Reed proved that Finlay had been right all along.

Mosquito control programs were immediately put in place in Cuba. Since mosquitoes lay eggs in standing pools of water, all standing water had to be treated. Any pool of water was ordered to be eliminated, or, if this was not possible, to be sprayed with a special oil that prevented mosquitoes from laying their eggs. The Cuban government took this so seriously that simply having water sitting around one's house was punishable with a five-dollar fine, which was considered a hefty price to pay.

As a result of these drastic measures, yellow fever disappeared from Cuba in only three months.

Even though it was Carlos Finlay who discovered that mosquitoes were responsible for the spread of the disease, it was Walter Reed who received the credit for beating yellow fever. Reed himself credited Finlay with the discovery in his own publications, but nobody bothered to listen.

Outside Cuba, Finlay's contributions were all but ignored. America went to war to help win Cuba's independence from the Spanish but came face to face with a deadlier enemy—yellow fever. Now, America could say that they won both wars. Admitting that Finlay, a Cuban, was behind the yellow fever discovery would weaken the view that America had won the war and that Cuba needed America. It would be a better tale of victory for America to hail Walter Reed the hero. The Walter Reed National Military Medical Center today bears his name and is the most prestigious military hospital in America.

Inside Cuba, however, Finlay was considered a hero. He was appointed chief sanitation officer, a well-respected, top-level government position. He held this post until his retirement. Finlay was also nominated for the Nobel Prize several times, though he never won the award. In 1908,

IN 1908, HE RECEIVED THE LEGION OF HONOR AWARD FROM FRANCE.

he received the Legion of Honor award from France. This is one of France's highest honors that is bestowed for significant contributions to the greater good of the world.

But since Carlos Juan Finlay loved his native Cuba so deeply, perhaps one of the most important honors bestowed upon him is a memorial that stands in the country's capital. The rest of the world may have ignored the contributions of Dr. Carlos Juan Finlay, but Cuba has not.

THERE ARE MANY KINDS of viruses. Some viruses, like the common cold, aren't very serious. Most people who catch a cold feel better in a few days. But other viruses can be deadly. Yellow fever is a type of virus that can be very dangerous to infected humans.

Viruses can spread from person to person in several different ways. Some viruses spread when an infected person coughs or sneezes, sending tiny droplets contaminated with the virus out into the air. A healthy person might breathe in this airborne droplet or might touch a surface,

like a table, contaminated with the droplet. A few days later, they may find themselves not feeling so great.

While many viruses are transmitted from person to person this way, other viruses, like yellow fever, take a different path to infect their host. These viruses require a vector to spread the disease. A vector is a living organism that spreads a virus. For yellow fever, the vector is the mosquito. More precisely, the female mosquito. How does this work? We've all been bitten by pesky mosquitoes and know how annoying that can be. When a mosquito bites someone infected by yellow fever, it takes a tiny bit of the person's blood. It takes the yellow fever virus along with the blood. The virus then incubates in the mosquito for approximately twelve days. After this incubation period, the mosquito can then pass along the yellow fever virus to everyone else it bites. For the rest of the mosquito's life, which is usually a few months, it can spread the virus to every human it comes into contact with. Not only that, but a mother mosquito can also pass along the virus to her eggs. When the baby mosquitoes hatch, they, too, can transmit the virus.

Scientists have developed vaccines for many deadly viruses like yellow fever. These vaccines provide immunity against the virus. If someone vaccinated with the yellow fever vaccine were to be bitten by a mosquito infected with the disease, their body would immediately respond and fight off the illness. Vaccines are the best defense in protecting us from dangerous viruses.

ANNA WESSELS WILLIAMS

1863–1954

When Anna Williams was a young girl growing up in New Jersey, she probably never dreamed she would grow up to save the world from one of the deadliest disease epidemics of the twentieth century. In fact, young Anna Williams likely didn't understand what a scientist was capable of. Williams was homeschooled until she was old enough to attend the public middle school. There, for the very first time, she got the chance to use a microscope. She was hooked. Thus began Williams's lifelong journey of exploration and the search for solutions to difficult problems.

Williams began her career as a teacher, but a family tragedy forced her to rethink her professional path. Her sister nearly died while giving birth. The baby, sadly, did not survive. Williams was heartbroken and angry. She believed the tragedy could have been avoided if medical professionals had more knowledge and better training. Rather than sit around complaining all day, Williams decided to do something about it. She quit her teaching job and enrolled in medical school. Medical school was a very unusual path for women at that time, but Williams believed that she deserved the same opportunity to study medicine as any man.

A few years later, Williams earned her medical degree. It was time for her to begin her medical career, except there was one thing she had a hard time getting past. Williams wanted to become a doctor to help sick people get better. The problem was, there were so many diseases for which there was no cure. How could she help her sick patients if there was no treatment? Once again, Williams decided to do something about it. Instead of becoming a practicing doctor, she would become a research scientist and devote her life to finding cures.

Williams decided to volunteer her time at the New York City Department of Health. There she worked for a man by the name of William Park, who was the director of the department. The year was 1894, and it was a busy time at the Department of Health. A disease named diphtheria was sweeping through the city and was nearing epidemic levels. Diphtheria spread from an infected person through their sneezes or coughs. At first, the symptoms of diphtheria are similar to those of a common cold, but after a few days, it begins to attack the sick person's organs. Without an effective treatment, most people infected with diphtheria die. Children at the time were particularly at risk.

Williams quickly got to work studying the diphtheria bacteria. She was only a volunteer, but she was determined to find a solution to the disease sweeping not only New York, but also the entire world. Just a few short months later, she had a breakthrough. She isolated a strain of the disease that made it possible to produce the diphtheria antitoxin. Her boss, William Park, was on vacation and not around to celebrate Williams's important discovery.

SHE ISOLATED A STRAIN OF THE DISEASE THAT MADE IT POSSIBLE TO PRODUCE THE DIPHTHERIA ANTITOXIN.

Nevertheless, even though Park wasn't there for the discovery, Williams didn't think excluding her boss would be an honorable thing to do. The strain discovered by Williams was named Park-Williams no. 8. Yet over time, the name became too long and cumbersome for people to say. Eventually, this important discovery became colloquially known just as Park 8.

Despite not getting the credit Williams deserved for her discovery, she was thrilled at the success of Park 8. Before the antitoxin, more than 100,000 people in the United States got sick from the disease every year, and nearly 15,000 people died. The antitoxin was mass-produced and shipped across the United States and then the world. Because of her discovery, the spread of diphtheria was halted. Today, fewer than five people in the United States get diphtheria every year, and for those who are infected, there are highly effective treatments available.

And this was all thanks to a discovery by Anna Williams, who did not receive the credit and accolades she deserved. She was, however, finally given a promotion at the Department of Health. She was no longer just a volunteer. Her new title was assistant bacteriologist. This title hardly seemed worthy for someone whose discoveries led to the cure for a terrifying disease. Williams, however, wasn't terribly offended. She still had important work to do.

Having solved the diphtheria problem, she got to work trying to crack the mysteries of another disease: rabies. Rabies is a disease caused by a virus that is usually spread by a bite or scratch from an infected animal. The biggest challenge treating someone infected with rabies is that by the time symptoms appear, it is usually too late. For the treatment to work, it must be given before symptoms appear. That's why diagnosing a patient with the rabies virus as quickly as possible is so important.

Williams had an idea. She knew that the rabies virus attacks the infected person's brain. She started looking for evidence of the disease in human brains, and there she found what she was looking for. An infected person's brain had specific cells that would make diagnosing the rabies virus quickly a possibility. The quick diagnosis would help save lives because treatment could begin before the onset of symptoms.

As is often the case in science, multiple scientists in different laboratories may be researching similar topics. Around the same time that Williams was studying rabies infected patients, a scientist in Italy was performing similar work. Williams may have discovered these cells, but before she was ready to make the important announcement, she wanted to double- and triple-check her results. While making sure her discovery was sound, the Italian researcher raced to publish his results. His name was Adelchi Negri. Williams may have been the first to observe the cells, but Negri was the first to publish. The cells are now known as Negri bodies.

Once again, Williams could not take credit for her discovery.

Williams was still not discouraged. There was still important work to be done. The problem of rabies was not completely solved. The Negri bodies were critical in diagnosing the disease, but the process could still take up to ten days. For rabies, starting a treatment plan as quickly as possible is key. Time is of the essence in diagnosing the disease. A year after the discovery of the Negri bodies, Williams discovered a way to instantly detect the rabies virus. With her discovery, instead of waiting ten days to diagnose the disease, a doctor could have test results in a half hour. Williams published her findings. Her method became the standard way for doctors to identify rabies in their patients for the next thirty years.

Williams went on to study other diseases, including flu, pneumonia, meningitis, and smallpox. As long as people got sick from horrible diseases, she would work to find cures. She published many papers and even wrote a medical textbook with her boss, William Park. She was still hard at work when, together with nearly one hundred other workers, she was forced to retire by the mayor of New York because they were over the age of seventy. She wasn't ready to stop working, but she had no choice. Anna Williams may not have had the same recognition as her male colleagues, but her research was critical in solving the problem of dangerous diseases of her time.

IN THE 1920s, DIPHTHERIA was a horrible disease that infected and killed many people. Today, this disease has been mostly eliminated, thanks to a diphtheria vaccine. In America, young children begin receiving the diphtheria vaccine when they are a few months old. For the vaccine to be effective, babies need a few doses, so doctors recommend multiple doses over the course of several months for full immunity. Ninety-five percent of people with up-to-date diphtheria vaccines are completely protected from the disease.

To help make administering vaccines easier for doctors and their patients, the diphtheria vaccine is combined with vaccines for two other diseases, tetanus and pertussis. These three vaccines are given to children as a powerhouse cocktail called DTaP, which stands for—you guessed it—"diphtheria, tetanus, and pertussis."

A DTaP vaccine works by "tricking" the body into producing an antitoxin for diphtheria. When the body has produced this antitoxin, it is able to completely fight off the disease if ever that person is exposed to it. To make a vaccine, scientists use chemicals to "inactivate" the diphtheria toxin. This dead toxin is called a "toxoid." You can't get sick by coming into contact with the toxoid, but the toxoid looks enough like the toxin in diphtheria to tell your immune system to make the antitoxin against the disease. Immunity achieved!

Most vaccines are given to a patient by a doctor via an injection. Nobody likes getting shots, but the diseases they prevent can be very serious and can last much longer than the temporary annoyance of a shot.

NETTIE STEVENS

1861–1912

For centuries, nobody understood why babies were born with male parts, female parts, or a mixture of both. There were all sorts of wild ideas. Some people thought it had to do with the kind of food the mother ate while she was pregnant. Other people theorized it had something to do with the surrounding temperature of the mother during pregnancy. But all these theories were complete nonsense. There is something on the *inside* that determines a person's assigned gender at birth. That something is called a chromosome. And we have a woman named Nettie Stevens to thank for that discovery.

After working as a teacher in her home state of Vermont for more than ten years, Nettie finally saved up enough money to attend Stanford University in California. By then, Nettie was thirty-five years old. Many people figured thirty-five years old was way too old to travel all the way across the country, start college, and pursue a career, but then again, most people back then didn't believe a woman should have a career at all, let alone a career in the sciences. A woman aspiring to be a scientist was quite unusual. Nettie Stevens was not discouraged. She earned both her bachelor's and master's degrees in science by the year 1900.

MOST PEOPLE BACK THEN DIDN'T BELIEVE A WOMAN SHOULD HAVE A CAREER AT ALL, LET ALONE A CAREER IN THE SCIENCES.

After Stanford, Nettie continued her studies, eventually earning a doctorate from Bryn Mawr, a women's college in Pennsylvania. This was a level of education that was very rare for women of the time. Nettie Stevens was now officially Dr. Stevens.

After earning her doctorate, Nettie set her sights on figuring out what determined birth gender. She built a lab at Bryn Mawr and performed scientific experiments trying to solve the mystery of birth gender determination. Ironically, even though Bryn Mawr was a women's college, it would be two men affiliated with the university who would shape the course of Nettie Stevens's legacy.

Edmund Beecher Wilson left his position as the chairman of the biology department at Bryn Mawr to continue his research at Columbia University. Even though he was no longer working at Bryn Mawr, he kept close ties with the university and frequently collaborated on important research. He even helped Bryn Mawr hire his replacement, a man named Thomas Hunt Morgan. Morgan would eventually become Nettie Stevens's teacher and later her research colleague.

Nettie Stevens worked very hard researching what determined birth gender. She made a breakthrough in 1905 studying mealworms. You might think the idea of playing with mealworms all day at work sounds gross, and maybe it was, but these critters helped Stevens make a profound discovery. Stevens examined the cells of the mealworms, or, more specifically, their chromosomes. A chromosome is found in the nucleus, or center, of every cell. Chromosomes define all the characteristics of an organism. In other words, the chromosomes work together, like a blueprint, to define how an animal or human works.

Chromosomes always come in pairs. Humans have twenty-three pairs of chromosomes, but the mealworms studied by Nettie Stevens have twenty pairs of chromosomes. Stevens observed that female mealworms have twenty large chromosomes. These two larger chromosomes paired together are usually referred to as XX. Male mealworms also have twenty chromosomes, but the twentieth chromosome was much smaller than all the other chromosomes. This smaller chromosome is usually referred to as Y, so when paired with the larger chromosome, it is referred to as XY. This smaller chromosome, found only in male mealworms, was an interesting finding. Was it possible this XY combination found only in the male mealworm could have something to do with birth gender determination?

It turns out, Nettie Stevens was on to something really big.

Around the same time that Nettie Stevens made her discovery at Bryn Mawr, Edmund Beecher Wilson was performing similar research at Columbia University. There is no disputing that Wilson was a brilliant scientist performing important work. Because of his contributions to science, a lot of people believe it was Wilson who discovered the role of XX and XY chromosomes. But even though Wilson's results were similar to those of Nettie Stevens, Wilson still held on to the belief that environmental factors played some role in birth gender determination. Stevens's research on the subject was more accurate than Wilson's.

Some people point to a published research paper by Wilson that supposedly proves he was first to discover the connection between chromosomes and birth gender, not Nettie Stevens. But this very same research paper included a footnote written by Wilson that says otherwise. In this footnote, Wilson stated that he was aware of Stevens's scientific discovery, and he went on to thank her for allowing him, Wilson, to refer to her results. In other words, Wilson himself proclaimed in his own published scientific paper that Stevens made the breakthrough discovery, not him.

Despite being a woman in a profession mostly of men, the scientific community of the time began taking notice of Nettie Stevens. In 1910, Stevens was profiled in the edition of *American Men of Science*. As silly as it is to think of a woman as a "man of science," this was a great honor, ranking Stevens as one of the top scientists of her time.

And while some scientists at the time were starting to become more convinced that chromosomes determined birth gender, others challenged this new school of thought. Thomas Hunt Morgan, Stevens's colleague at Bryn Mawr, remained skeptical. Morgan didn't think that Stevens provided enough scientific proof. Stevens, under pressure, suggested that animal breeding experiments could offer this unquestionable proof that Morgan was demanding.

Stevens was right. Breeding experiments did, in fact, prove that chromosomes determined gender assigned at birth. Guess who settled the matter?

Thomas Hunt Morgan.

By conducting breeding experiments, as suggested by Stevens, Morgan built upon Stevens's research and proved that it was, indeed, chromosomes alone that determined gender assigned at birth. For his contribution, Morgan was awarded the Nobel Prize.

Morgan never bothered to thank Nettie Stevens for her groundbreaking work, which helped pave the way for his own research. On the contrary, Morgan publicly mocked Stevens's scientific research. He called her overcautious and made her out to be more of a lab technician than an accomplished scientist.

Dr. Nettie Stevens did not live to see Thomas Hunt Morgan further her own research and win the Nobel Prize. She died of cancer at the age of fifty-one, only a few short years after her scientific discovery. Despite the fact that her research was never publicly acknowledged, at a time when women couldn't even vote, Dr. Nettie Stevens made a profound impact on the scientific research community, paving the way for future breakthroughs in medical and biological sciences.

IF YOU EVER WONDERED why you might have your mother's eye color but your father's hair color, the answer is genetics. Genetics is the science that studies heredity. Heredity explains how traits are passed down between generations. These traits are determined by genes. A gene is a segment of genetic material that controls a specific trait. Genes are what make you uniquely you.

Genes are very small and cannot be seen without extremely powerful microscopes. They are found on structures called chromosomes. Each chromosome may contain hundreds or thousands of different genes that define who you are, what you look like, how your brain operates, your blood type, your favorite hobbies, your best subjects, and so much more!

In most cases, humans inherit twenty-three chromosomes from their mother and twenty-three chromosomes from their father. Together, humans have a total of forty-six chromosomes. Each chromosome inherited from one parent pairs up with the corresponding chromosome inherited from the other parent. The pairs are similar to each other and have the same size and shape. These two corresponding chromosomes that pair together are called homologous pairs. Each homologous pair carries the same gene type at the same location, but the genes themselves on each of the chromosomes don't have to be the same. For example, on the chromosome you inherited from your mother, you may have the gene for green eyes. At the very same location on the corresponding chromosome that you inherited from your father, you may have the gene for brown eyes. Even though you have the same type of genetic information, the gene for eye color, at the same location on both pairs of chromosomes, the genes themselves are different. So, will you have green eyes or brown eyes? That will depend on which gene is dominant and how the two genes combine. You will have the trait of the more dominant characteristic.

Chromosomes that determine someone's birth gender are special cases. The other forty-four chromosomes combine into homologous pairs, but the chromosomes that determine birth gender are not homologous. They are different and carry different genetic information. These chromosomes can be either X chromosomes or Y chromosomes. Birth gender is determined by how the X and Y chromosomes pair up. If two X chromosomes combine (XX), a baby with female parts will

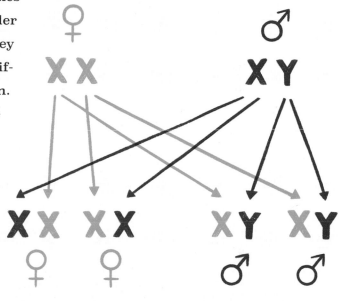

be born. If an X and a Y chromosome combine (XY), a baby with male parts will be born. The mother always passes an X chromosome to her child, because that's the only chromosome she has. The father, however, can pass either an X chromosome or a Y chromosome to his child. Whether a child gets an X or a Y chromosome from their father is totally random.

LISE MEITNER

Lise Meitner was born in Austria and was one of eight children in her family. She was always smart and always wanted to learn, but Austria restricted women from many educational opportunities. Women in Austria were not allowed to attend college, but her family paid for her to receive a private education. She then went to the University of Vienna for graduate school. She was only the second woman to ever earn a doctorate degree in physics from the institution. This was already an impressive accomplishment for Lise Meitner. But the young Austrian woman wanted more. She wanted to be a real scientist. The problem was there weren't many prospects for women in Austria looking to become research scientists, especially in the growing field of physics. Meitner's career options would be limited to teaching, and this just wouldn't do. If she ever wanted to be a real physicist, Meitner would have to leave Austria.

Meitner decided her best chances of landing a position in a physics lab would be in Berlin, Germany. A lot of notable scientists were already working there, publishing exciting research that was taking the physics world by storm. Berlin was where the action was, and Meitner wanted in on that action. But it wasn't easy for a young woman to pick up and move her life to another country. For one thing, she didn't have the money. She was still being supported financially by her parents. Meitner decided to ask her parents to allow her to travel to Berlin, where she hoped there would be more opportunities for a smart, hardworking scientist.

Meitner's parents agreed to the arrangement. In 1907, at the age of twenty-eight, Lise Meitner left her home country of Austria and moved to Berlin. Meitner figured she would only be in Germany for a short while, but, as it turned out, she would never set foot back in Austria again.

Meitner's research interests were in the budding field of radioactivity. Shortly after her arrival at the University of Berlin, she met a chemist named Otto Hahn, who was also investigating radioactivity. As a chemist, Hahn was an expert at preparing the chemicals for his experiments and conducting the chemical reactions in the lab, but he needed help explaining the math and physics behind his results. In came Meitner, who was an expert at understanding physics but didn't have the knowledge to carry out the chemical experiments. It was a perfect partnership. Meitner needed Hahn's chemistry skills, and Hahn needed Meitner's physics skills. The two decided to get to work.

But there was one big problem. The chairman of the chemistry department at the university, a man named Emil Fischer, did not allow women to enter his labs. He feared women working in a chemistry lab would run the risk of setting their hair on fire (of course, he never feared his own bushy beard would ignite). Meitner was forbidden from working in the same lab as her male research partner. Otto Hahn helped Meitner set up a lab in the university's basement. Meitner was often shamed by members of the chemistry department. When colleagues would walk past Hahn and Meitner together, they would usually address Hahn alone—"Good day, Herr Hahn"—and completely ignore Meitner.

But while the chemistry department at the University of Berlin did everything to insult and demean Lise Meitner, the physics community in Berlin was welcoming and supportive. Meitner would often socialize with prominent physicists of the time, like Max Planck and Albert Einstein. Einstein held Meitner in high regard, often fondly calling her "our Madam Curie," a nod to one of the most famous female scientists of that time, Marie Curie.

Life in Berlin was challenging for Lise Meitner, but she was doing what she loved more than anything else in the world: experimenting with science. She grew to love Berlin, her university position, and her scientist friends. Up until then, the biggest discrimination she faced was being a woman working in a man's field. It was certainly unpleasant, but Meitner was strong and was able to look past the biases. However, soon she would face a far more serious discrimination: being Jewish in Nazi Germany.

For several years, Meitner worked under the Nazi government with increasing restrictions. At first, Meitner wasn't too worried. She figured there wasn't much the German government could do to her since she wasn't German. She was Austrian. Her friend Albert Einstein, also a Jewish scientist in Germany, wasn't as confident. He feared for what was to come and decided to move his family out of Germany to America while he still had the chance. Meitner, however, decided it was safe to stay put and continue working on the science she loved.

In April 1933, the Nazi government decided that all people with at least one Jewish grandparent had to declare their Jewish ancestry and be labeled as "non-Aryan." Meitner completed the paperwork. Then, it was announced that all people of Jewish descent would be removed from university and government positions. Meitner still wasn't too worried. She assumed she could hold on to her job despite the new German policies. She was confident her Austrian citizenship would protect her.

In 1938, Germany seized control of Austria. The land of Austria became part of the German Empire. Lise Meitner, who had always counted on her Austrian citizenship to shield her against the rising Nazi party, was now worried. She decided that for her own safety, it was time to leave Germany.

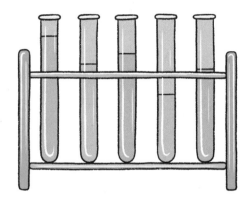

Leaving Germany wasn't that simple. She had an Austrian passport, which was worthless now that Austria was part of Germany. Austria didn't exist anymore. She couldn't apply for a German passport, because she was Jewish and that was forbidden. She couldn't even get approval to leave Germany to visit another country, even for a short vacation. This is because the German government worried that scientists traveling to other countries would give away German discoveries and German secrets. Meitner was, by then, a fairly well-regarded scientist, and even though she was Jewish, the Germans did not want to lose what they considered to be their scientific superiority.

Meitner was desperate. The situation grew worse and worse for the Jewish people in Germany. She feared for her life. With encouragement from her friend and partner, Otto Hahn, she decided she had no choice but to run away in secret. This was an illegal act. She knew fleeing would be very dangerous, but the situation was dire. She packed only a few suitcases of clothes and left most of her other possessions behind. Under the cover of night and with the help of friends and kind border guards, she managed to sneak out of the country.

Meitner settled in Stockholm, Sweden. She missed Berlin and the research she had been working on in her lab, but at least she was finally safe. While in exile in Stockholm, she often exchanged letters with her friend, Otto Hahn, who stayed back in Germany. She encouraged Hahn to continue with the science experiments they had been working on together before she was forced to flee. They were performing tests on uranium, a chemical element, which was showing interesting properties. Meitner didn't have the equipment to perform any experiments in Stockholm, but she coached Hahn from afar, sending letters back and forth.

With inspiration and support from Meitner, Hahn continued testing uranium. He was trying to prove that bombarding uranium with subatomic particles called neutrons would create a new, heavier element. But Hahn's results were surprising. The resulting elements were actually lighter, not heavier. Hahn couldn't make sense of this. How was it possible that adding neutrons to uranium made lighter elements instead of heavier ones?

Hahn, stumped by what he was seeing in the lab, wrote to Meitner in Stockholm. It was Meitner, in collaboration with her nephew Otto Frisch, who figured out what was happening. Bombarding uranium with neutrons actually causes the atom to split apart. Meitner then used her old friend Albert Einstein's famous formula, $E=MC^2$, to show that when the atom splits apart, it releases a lot of energy. They called this process fission.

Shortly thereafter, in 1939, Meitner and Frisch published their discovery of fission in a journal of science, *Nature*. They explained that fission happens when an atom separates and creates energy. When this paper was published, it caused many physicists to worry. They feared that the energy created as a result of fission could be very dangerous. Scientists feared, especially with the rise of Nazi power throughout Europe, that the energy could be used to build a destructive weapon: an atomic bomb. Knowing the German enemy had the knowledge to create an atomic bomb, scientists in the United States decided to act. They approached Albert Einstein and convinced him to write a letter to President Roosevelt, warning him of the dangers. Albert Einstein was already a famous scientist, and they figured if anyone had a shot at convincing Roo-sevelt to take action, it would be a celebrity like Einstein.

It worked. Einstein's letter alarmed Roosevelt enough that he ordered the formation of the Manhattan Project, a top-secret initiative to research, design, and build an atomic bomb. The goal? Beat the enemy to the weapon. It came as no surprise that Lise Meitner, the scientist who discovered fission, was asked to join the Manhattan Project team in America. Meitner refused the invitation. She wanted nothing to do with building an atomic bomb.

SHE WANTED NOTHING TO DO WITH BUILDING AN ATOMIC BOMB.

Otto Hahn also published the story of the splitting of the atom and the fission process. On his publication he did not include Meitner's name or any mention that Meitner assisted in the groundbreaking scientific discovery. He never revealed that it was Meitner who explained the theory behind what Hahn had observed in his lab. Some people think Hahn didn't give credit to Meitner because of her Jewish heritage, which, at the peak of Nazi rule, would have immediately discredited the research. Whatever the reason, Meitner's contribution to the discovery of fission was all but ignored. Hahn would go on to win the Nobel Prize in 1944 for the discovery that should have been shared with his longtime partner and friend, Lise Meitner.

Despite the Nobel Prize snub, in 1966 Lise Meitner and Otto Hahn were awarded the prestigious Fermi Prize for their discovery of fission. While this award does not carry the prestige of the Nobel Prize, it was still a great honor. But perhaps the biggest honor bestowed upon Lise Meitner, a scientist who devoted her life to studying the properties of radioactive elements, was a radioactive element of her own. In 1997, element number 109 was named meitnerium in Meitner's honor. Lise Meitner will forever hold a spot on the periodic table of elements.

NUCLEAR ENERGY IS THE energy stored in the center, or nucleus, of an atom. Atoms make up everything in the universe. The process of breaking atoms apart is called fission. Fission works when tiny particles called neutrons collide with an atom of uranium. There are several different forms of uranium atoms with slightly different masses. The different uranium atoms are called isotopes. Few isotopes can undergo fission, and uranium-235 requires the least energy to do so. The number 235 represents the mass of this specific uranium isotope.

In a nuclear reaction, neutrons collide with a uranium-235 atom. When a neutron hits the nucleus of the atom, the uranium-235 becomes uranium-236. This new uranium-236 isotope is unstable. It can't stay in this form for very long, so it bursts apart. When the atom splits, it releases additional neutrons and a lot of energy. These new neutrons can then hit other uranium atoms, setting off a chain reaction. The chain reaction will go on and on until all the uranium gets used up. If there was enough uranium in the reactor, the reaction could be massive.

The energy that is released every time an atom undergoes fission can be explained with Albert Einstein's formula, $E=MC^2$. In this equation E stands for energy, M stands for mass, and C is a number that represents the speed of light. This formula shows that a large amount of energy can be produced from a very small amount of matter. In the case of nuclear fission, a large amount of energy can be produced from a small amount of uranium.

Nuclear energy relies on the chain reaction of the uranium atoms splitting. With enough uranium, the chain reaction grows bigger and bigger and would, eventually, grow large enough to cause an enormous explosion. The atomic bomb is an example of a nuclear chain reaction with a huge amount of destructive energy.

Fission isn't only used for destructive purposes. Nuclear energy produced as a result of fission can be used to generate electricity in a power plant. Nuclear power is very efficient. For example, a very small amount of uranium is able to produce as much electricity as 150 gallons of oil.

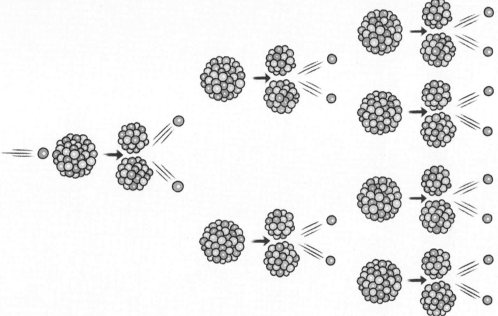

A lot of people consider nuclear power to be a good alternative energy source. But nuclear power plants do have risks. Left unchecked, chain reactions in a nuclear reactor can grow and cause a "meltdown." These meltdowns are extremely dangerous. That's why it's important that nuclear power plants take special precautions to ensure safe operations.

ALICE BALL

1892–1916

In the early 1900s, before Hawaii had become an official state, a man named Harry Hollmann worked as a treating physician at Kalihi Hospital. Dr. Hollmann's job was one of the most dismaying assignments in the hospital. He would receive and treat patients plagued with leprosy, a frightening disease.

Though today leprosy is easily treated, it has terrified people since ancient times. Leprosy is a disease of the skin. Symptoms often include sores and loss of feeling in the arms and legs. A lot of people associated leprosy with disfigurement, even though this wasn't an actual symptom of the disease. Infected people were often depicted with rotting flesh or severed body parts.

It's no surprise, then, that people suffering from leprosy were almost always teased and tormented. In some places, infected people were ordered to wear bells so others would know they were approaching and could get out of the way. In other places, infected people were forced to live far away from the rest of society in areas called "leper colonies."

Thousands of leprosy patients came through the doors of Kalihi Hospital. Hollmann did his best to treat the patients, but if the disease was too advanced or considered incurable Hollmann had no other choice but to exile patients to a leper colony on the Hawaiian island of Molokai. There, they would live far away from their families, isolated from the rest of society, never to be seen again. The families would hold funerals for their banished relatives even though they were still living.

Patients were offered all kinds of experimental treatments for leprosy. Some of the treatments were horribly painful, while others caused severe nausea. None of the treatments worked. Dr. Hollmann needed something better to help his patients.

Hollmann was optimistic that he might be able to cure his patients with a special kind of oil that had been used for centuries by healers in Asia to treat leprosy. This oil, called chaulmoogra oil, came from the seeds of the chaulmoogra tree. The oil proved to be effective in treating leprosy, but only sometimes. It wasn't reliable, and it was very difficult to work with. When used as an ointment applied directly to the skin, it gave limited relief to the symptoms. When patients swallowed the oil, they would get sick to their stomachs. If injected, the oil was so thick and sticky that it just sat in a blob under the skin and did nothing.

Hollmann guessed that his best chance to help his patients would be to find a better way to inject the oil. He needed to find a way to help the thick, oozy oil travel through the patient's body. The best medicine would have the active component of the oil in a thinned-out form. This is much harder than it sounds. He couldn't simply add water to the oil to make it less thick. Water and oil don't mix very well. They separate from each other.

Hollmann needed help from a chemist to solve this problem. He knew of a young graduate student named Alice Ball at the College of Hawaii who had performed similar work. Ball was only in her early twenties but already had an impressive list of accomplishments. She was the first African American woman to earn an undergraduate degree at the college, and also became the first woman to ever earn a master's degree in chemistry there. After she earned her degrees, the university hired her as a teacher.

Hollmann asked Alice Ball for help and she agreed. She immediately got to work. She did her research on the chaulmoogra oil in her spare time, around her full-time teaching responsibilities. It took her less than a year, but Ball found a way to extract the active ingredients in the oil and create a safe, injectable version with minimal side effects.

And Ball's injection worked! Patients sent to Kalihi Hospital were treated with the oil injection and were shortly thereafter discharged—to their homes and their families, not to the leper colony.

Sadly, Ball never had a chance to publish her results. Soon after her work on the injectable chaulmoogra, she got sick and died. She was only twenty-four years old. The president of the College of Hawaii, a man named Arthur Dean, published Ball's research without giving Ball any credit. In fact, he called the discovery the "Dean Method."

Dr. Hollmann wasn't content to sit back and let Ball's work go unrecognized. A few years later he published a paper in a medical journal, trying to set the record straight. He referred to the cure as the "Ball Method."

Despite Hollmann's attempt to

HE REFERRED TO THE CURE AS THE "BALL METHOD."

correct the record, Ball's contribution to the cure of leprosy went mostly unrecognized for over ninety years. And then, in 2000, the College of Hawaii, now called the University of Hawaii, recognized this unsung hero. They placed a bronze plaque in front of the only chaulmoogra tree that remained on campus, with an inscription dedicated to Alice Ball and her work. On that same day, the lieutenant governor of Hawaii declared February 29 Alice Ball Day. Leprosy today is now called Hansen's disease. It is completely curable.

What's the SCIENCE?

WHEN YOU'RE SICK OR feeling lousy, you rely on medicine to help you feel better. Today, a lot of medicine is manufactured in a laboratory where chemicals can be combined in just the right way to target a specific illness. But historically, before the days of modern medicine, people would use remedies found in nature to help them feel better. Sometimes this would be a plant, flower, or twig that people discovered, often by accident, to soothe or cure an ailment.

Even today, scientists still study home remedies to create better drugs and medical treatments. They look at *why* a particular leaf, flower, or weed provides relief for a symptom. If they can identify the exact component in nature that acts like a medicine, they can extract the active ingredient to make more effective treatments. For example, bark from willow trees has been used for centuries as a pain reliever. Ancient people didn't know why willow bark made them feel better; they just knew it did. Scientists looked carefully at the makeup of the willow bark to isolate the specific component responsible for relieving people's pain symptoms. They found that one component, acetylsalicylic acid, was the source of the pain reliever. Scientists were then able to extract this component to produce aspirin. Today, aspirin is one of the most widely used pain relievers, but it is all thanks to an ingredient found in nature.

Chaulmoogra oil, taken from the seed of the chaulmoogra tree, had been used for centuries to relieve the symptoms of leprosy, but it was never a reliable cure. It worked sometimes, but not all the time. The theory was that for a cure to be reliably effective, scientists would need to find a way to inject the active ingredient in the oil into a patient's body and allow the medicine to circulate through the patient's bloodstream. The problem was the oil was very thick, making it impossible to inject. The oil could not be thinned by water because oil does not mix with water.

For an effective leprosy cure, Alice Ball had to find a way to isolate a specific ingredient from the chaulmoogra oil, then find a way for that

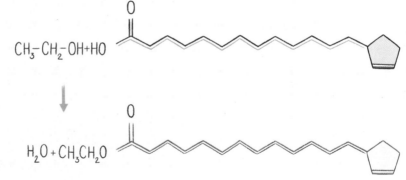

ingredient to circulate through a patient's body. To accomplish this, she turned to chemistry. She discovered that the fatty acids in the oil, when exposed to an alcohol, produce something called an ethyl ester. Ethyl esters are soluble in water. Using chemistry, Alice Ball was able to extract the active ingredient from the chaulmoogra oil, dissolve it in water, and create an injectable, effective medicine to treat leprosy.

HILDE MANGOLD

1898-1924

Hilde Mangold wasn't a mad scientist when she created a two-headed amphibian in her laboratory. She wasn't trying to invent some monstrous creature. Mangold was actually performing groundbreaking science.

Shortly after the end of World War I, Hilde Mangold was a young researcher working in a lab at the University of Freiburg in Germany. Her advisor was an admired scientist by the name of Hans Spemann. Spemann and his graduate students were performing important research in the field of biology. Mangold was thrilled to be working with such esteemed members of the science community as she worked to earn her PhD degree.

Except, Spemann didn't treat all his students equally. While Mangold's male colleagues were assigned to exciting research projects, Spemann asked her to replicate an experiment that was successfully proved two hundred years earlier. Why would a scientist hoping to make new discoveries want to waste her time on a science project that was performed two hundred years ago? While the men in the lab were performing cutting-edge science, Mangold was doing little more than grunt work. And it wasn't just Mangold who was subjected to this level of humiliation. Other female students tolerated similar discrimination working for Spemann. The women were frequently assigned the most boring research assignments in the lab.

Eventually, Mangold asked Spemann to reassign her to another project. Spemann agreed and gave her a project that would help support his own research in embryology. Embryology is a subject in biology that studies the way complex living creatures develop from a single cell. Humans, and all animals, start life as nothing more than a collection of cells. In the very early stages of development, these tiny cell groups are called embryos. Eventually, these cells duplicate and divide into a fully formed tiny living creature. Mangold was tasked to answer an important question about these embryos: how do cells "know" what to do? How does a part of the embryo know to grow into a heart or lung, while other parts of the embryo grow into arms or skin? This was the mystery Hilde Mangold set forth to solve.

She worked with embryos of newts—amphibian animals that look like a cross between a frog and a lizard. Newt embryos are tiny—no bigger than a single grain of sand. A high-powered microscope would have made her job so much simpler, but back in the early 1900s, when Mangold was performing her research, such instruments weren't invented yet. She had to do her work with a simple, low-powered microscope and makeshift lab instruments. To manipulate the tiny newt embryos, Mangold used a loop made out of an ultrafine strand of baby's hair. The baby who donated the lock of hair happened to be Hans Spemann's infant daughter.

While observing the newt embryos, Mangold noticed that as the embryo developed, a small section took on a sunken shape. Imagine you're holding a ball of clay and you press your thumb against the surface of one side. Where your thumb presses against the clay, a small indentation forms. This type of formation in embryos is called the dorsal lip. Mangold observed the dorsal lip while studying newt embryos under a microscope.

With extreme care and precision, she cut the dorsal lip away from the tiny embryo. She then implanted the cut-away sample onto the side of an entirely different newt embryo. This host embryo already had its own dorsal lip forming, so Mangold had to carefully select a spot on the opposite side so the donated dorsal lip wouldn't interfere with the dorsal lip that was already there. The resulting embryo now had two dorsal lips, one on each side.

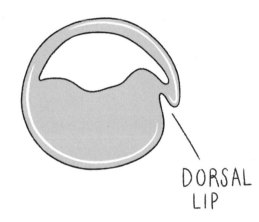

DORSAL LIP

The next step in the experiment was to wait and see how the tiny newt embryos would grow. But first, Mangold had to return the newt embryos to their natural growing environment, and for newts that would be pond water. The problem that Mangold soon encountered was that pond water contains a lot of germs and contaminants. The newt embryos handled by Mangold were frail, having just undergone a sensitive grafting process. If Mangold had had access to antibiotics to treat the pond water with, she could have assured the survival of the tiny embryos. But this was years before antibiotics was invented. Unfortunately, most of Mangold's samples died very quickly.

Mangold worked for two years to get six of the newt embryos to survive, and the resulting creatures were quite remarkable: The single newt embryo had grown into a pair of twin newts joined at the belly. The creature had two fully formed heads!

Mangold had proved that the dorsal lip was, indeed, the most important part of a developing embryo. This area was named the "organizer" because

MANGOLD HAD PROVED THAT THE DORSAL LIP WAS, INDEED, THE MOST IMPORTANT PART OF A DEVELOPING EMBRYO.

it is able to direct the growth of surrounding cells to form a fully functioning animal. When Mangold grafted the organizer onto the host embryo, she was very careful not to disrupt the organizer that was already there. The resulting embryo had two organizers and was able to direct the surrounding cells to form two newts.

Mangold wrote a paper about her work with newt embryos and submitted it to her advisor. She received a good, but not perfect, grade for her work. The paper was published in 1924 and became Mangold's PhD thesis paper. Despite all her hard work, Spemann insisted that his name be listed as an author on the paper. Not only that, but he also demanded that his name be listed before Mangold's. It is true that Spemann was Mangold's research advisor, offering her advice and mentoring for the two years she was studying the newt embryos—but, during this same time, there were many male PhD students working under Spemann's direction. All of them were permitted to publish their work without Spemann's name.

Eleven years after the publication of Hilde Mangold's paper, Hans

Spemann was awarded the Nobel Prize for the discovery of the organizer. This was the first time a PhD paper was used to award the prestigious Nobel award. That paper, of course, was authored by Hilde Mangold, with Spemann's name slapped on as the first author. Mangold died before she got to see her advisor take the credit for her research. She was killed in a horrible fire at the age of twenty-six. The Nobel Prize committee does not grant awards posthumously, so it's impossible to know if the committee considered awarding the prize to both Spemann and Mangold. After all, even though Spemann's name was first on the paper, Mangold's name was included as the second author. The Nobel committee did mention Mangold's thesis in their prize announcement, even if Spemann drastically minimized Mangold's role in his acceptance speech.

Today, the discovery made in the German lab by Hilde Mangold is widely known as the Spemann-Mangold Organizer. And while Spemann's name is, sadly, still noted as first, the young female scientist is beginning to get the recognition she deserves.

HISTORICALLY, A BIG DEBATE in the study of biology was whether early embryos that form in the womb of their mother are teeny versions of a person or something else. Some people argued that an embryo is basically an adult but in super miniature form. They believed that this early embryo already had a heart, brain, and everything else a human needs to survive. They argued that development of the embryo increases the size of the person-to-be until it is ready to be born. People called this theory "preformation"—in other words, an embryo was a preformed human.

On the other hand, other people argued that the early embryo is a collection of cells that have little resemblance to a human being. This

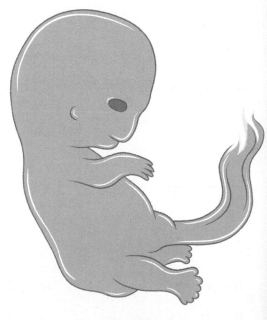

FERTILIZED
EGG

BLASTOCYST

4 WEEKS

8 WEEKS

theory states that development of the embryo would eventually form organs and body parts and can be considered a tiny human, but only after undergoing multiple developmental stages. This theory is called epigenesis.

Scientists proved that epigenesis was the correct theory that explained embryo development. It turns out it takes about eight weeks for a human embryo to divide, replicate, and grow into the basics of a little human. Once the embryo differentiates into everything a baby needs to survive, it is no longer called an embryo. It is now called a fetus. The fetus continues to grow in its mother's womb until it is strong enough to be born. For humans, a pregnancy is considered "full term" at nine months. This doesn't mean that all babies are born at exactly nine months. Some babies are born several weeks early. They might be smaller than a full-term baby, but with proper care they can be perfectly healthy.

How does a collection of cells in the embryo "know" how to organize itself into all the body parts needed to form a little human? It turns out the organizer discovered by Hilde Mangold "talks" with other tissues to direct development. The organizer is an example of a biological process called induction. Induction allows certain cells to influence the development of other, nearby cells. It is this induction process that provides the instructions to turn an embryo into a fully functioning baby.

CHIEN-SHIUNG WU

1912-1997

I n 1912, a mother and father in China welcomed the birth of their baby daughter. They named her Chien-Shiung Wu, which means "courageous hero" in Chinese. Perhaps Mr. and Mrs. Wu bestowed this bold name upon their daughter as a wish for her future. Or perhaps they hoped the name would eventually inspire their baby girl to greatness. Whatever the reason, Chien-Shiung Wu would grow up to embody her given name.

It wasn't easy for Wu as a smart little girl growing up in China. Back then, girls were discouraged from pursuing an education. Instead, proper girls of the time were taught to be dutiful and learn to run a household. Chien-Shiung Wu's parents did not agree with the customs of the time that said girls did not deserve an education. They knew their daughter was smart and wanted to give her every opportunity to learn. The problem was, there weren't many schools in China that educated girls. That wouldn't stop Mr. Wu. Since there wasn't a school for his daughter, he decided to start his own school. Her father opened the very first school for girls in the area.

Wu was a good student and excelled at her studies. But by the time she was ten years old, her parents realized there wasn't much else they could teach her. They had done all they could, but young Wu needed more. Her parents decided the best chance for their daughter to get the instruction she deserved was to send her away to a girls' boarding school fifty miles from her home. She then continued her education, studying physics at the university level. But she soon outgrew her university work, too.

Wu realized that to grow as a physicist, she would have no choice but to leave China and pursue her research in America. When she was twenty-four years old, she boarded a boat to America. Her destination was the University of Michigan, where she hoped to perform postgraduate physics research. Upon arriving in America, Wu learned that at the University of Michigan women were not allowed to use the front entrance. This didn't sit well with Wu. She hadn't come all the way to America to be treated so unfairly. Wu decided, instead, to attend the University of California, Berkeley where there were more opportunities for women researchers.

But unfortunately for Wu, she had many challenges. Even though Berkeley was considered an open-minded institution, she found it hard to be taken seriously as a woman in her chosen field of physics. It didn't help that English was tricky for her to master. She spoke with a heavy Chinese accent, had trouble pronouncing certain words, and sometimes made grammar mistakes. It was also a time in America where Asian people were heavily discriminated against, especially in the years leading up to the Pearl Harbor invasion by the Japanese. All this made life very difficult for the young physicist.

Despite the challenges Wu faced, she excelled as a researcher. In 1944, during the height of World War II, she was invited to work for a top secret program at Columbia University, code-named the Manhattan Project. The project's goal? To develop the most powerful weapon the world had ever seen: the atomic bomb. Wu's role on the Manhattan Project was to develop a process to enrich uranium to be used as fuel for an atomic bomb. She was the only Chinese person on the Manhattan Project team.

On August 6, 1945, Wu's work was revealed to the world when a uranium bomb was dropped on the city of Hiro-

SHE WAS THE ONLY CHINESE PERSON ON **THE MANHATTAN PROJECT** TEAM.

shima in Japan. Two days later, a second atomic bomb was dropped on the city of Nagasaki. To this day, the bombs dropped on Hiroshima and Nagasaki were the only times nuclear weapons have been used in combat. And while the effects were devastating, the bombings did finally put an end to the bloodiest war in history.

After the war, the Manhattan Project was no longer needed, but Wu decided to stay at Columbia University to continue her research in nuclear physics with a focus on beta decay. She became one of the leading experts in this field. Often other scientists would ask Wu for her advice to help solve thorny problems they were having with their own research. Two such scientists were men by the names of Tsung-Dao Lee and Chen Ning Yang. They were studying a widely accepted physics law called the principle of conservation parity. Lee and Yang believed this law may not apply to beta decay. They just needed someone to prove their theory, and they turned to Wu.

But in science, "laws" are considered hard facts, so proving a scientific law wrong is next to impossible. Before she set off on this task, she would need to be sure there was a possibility, even if it were very small, that the law would not hold under certain conditions. Once she had collected enough theoretical evidence that the law might not apply to certain subatomic particles under beta decay, she set off to prove it.

She designed a series of scientific experiments to disprove the law. She worked long hours for many months carrying out her experiments, often operating on only a few hours of sleep. She even decided to cancel a long-awaited trip to China to visit her parents. She could not sacrifice time away from the lab when she was so close to making a groundbreaking discovery. Sadly, her parents would die in the coming years, and Wu would not see them again.

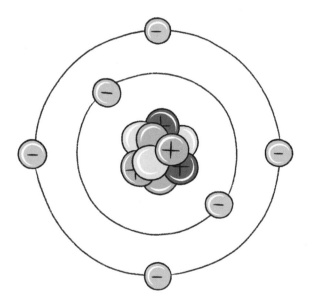

After months of dedication, hard work, and sacrifices, Wu's results were finally announced in the *New York Times*. The front-page story declared the "shattering of a fundamental concept of nuclear physics." She had accomplished what was once believed to be impossible. She had debunked a scientific law.

In 1957, the Nobel Prize committee decided to award the scientists for this groundbreaking discovery. They awarded the prize to Lee and Yang. Wu's hard work to disprove the conservation of parity theory went unacknowledged.

Despite the snub, Chien-Shiung Wu was awarded the Wolf Prize in Physics. This is regarded as the second-highest physics award after the Nobel Prize. She also had the distinct honor of having an asteroid named after her. But one of Wu's most notable contributions is the inspiration she provided to young girls looking to pursue careers in the sciences. Like her father, who shunned Chinese tradition and educated his young daughter, Chien-Shiung Wu believed every young girl deserved an opportunity to learn. She often traveled to speak about the importance of equal representation in science. She encouraged young girls to take inspiration from her work and to pursue careers in science and engineering. She provided lasting support for girls all over the world.

What's the SCIENCE?

EVERYTHING IN THE UNIVERSE is made up of small units called atoms. Atoms are also called elements. At the center of all atoms is the nucleus. The nucleus contains two particles called protons and neutrons. Adding the mass of the protons and neutrons together gives the atomic mass of the atom. The periodic table graphically shows every known atom arranged by increasing atomic mass.

Sometimes, the nucleus of an atom is unstable and undergoes a change. When a change happens in the nucleus, it might undergo radioactive decay. One type of radioactive decay is called beta decay. During

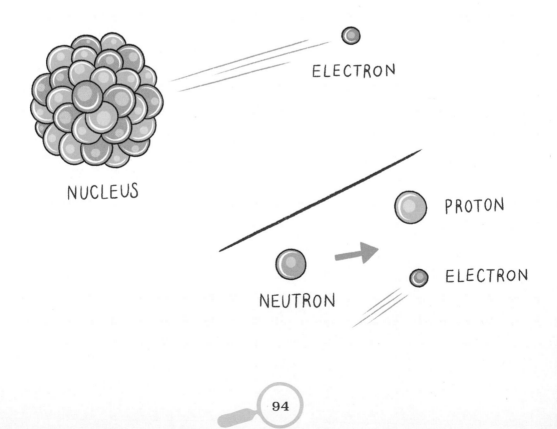

ELECTRON

NUCLEUS

PROTON

NEUTRON

ELECTRON

beta decay, one of the neutrons in the nucleus morphs into a proton. At the same time, a negatively charged electron is expelled from the atom. This causes energy in the form of radiation to be released from the atom. The element is then transformed into a completely different element altogether.

The law of conservation of parity, the widely accepted principal for decades, stated that nature does not favor left from right. Mirror images must behave identically. Conservation of parity can best be explained with an example. Imagine you are standing directly across from your friend. You hold a ball in your right hand. Your friend holds the identical ball in their left hand. You and your friend release the ball at the exact same moment from the exact same height. What happens? Both balls hit the ground precisely at the exact same moment. It doesn't matter that you released the ball from your right hand, and your friend performed the mirror image action. Nature doesn't care.

The same idea applies in the nucleus of decaying atoms. During beta decay, an equal number of electrons are discharged from one end of the atom as they are from the opposite end of the atom. That's what the law of conservation of parity demands, and this is the behavior that had been observed for decades—until a new subatomic particle called the K-meson was discovered. The K-meson violated everything scientists believed must hold true. It favored the release of electrons toward one end of the atom. Chien-Shiung Wu proved that in the case of K-mesons the conservation of parity theory did not apply.

MARIE THARP

1920–2006

As a young woman, Marie Tharp had already earned herself a college degree with a double major in English and music from Ohio University. These were two respectable degrees for a young woman of her time. But Marie Tharp found her chosen majors to be incredibly boring. She was interested in the sciences, but she knew a career in science was a long shot. Most universities at that time didn't admit women into their science programs.

But that all changed with the outbreak of World War II. Because most of the men were off fighting a war, universities realized that the only way to develop the next generation of scientists and engineers was to open the door to women. A year after the war started, the University of Michigan posted fliers encouraging young women to apply to their geology department. Geology is the study of the earth's features and formation. World

War II offered Tharp an opportunity she never imagined would be open to her—the opportunity to study science.

But Tharp knew it would be an uphill battle to excel as a geologist. Much of geology involves fieldwork. Even with a college degree, the chances of a woman landing a fieldwork job were pretty slim. Being a scientist was bad enough; being a scientist out in the field, crouching, wading, working with tools, getting dirty—well, that was hardly a suitable job for a proper lady. Knowing the challenges Tharp would face as a geologist, her mentors encouraged her to work on her drafting and drawing skills. They figured this would improve her chances of getting any kind of job as a geologist. With drafting skills, she could at least have a chance at finding work behind a desk, drawing the results collected by men out in the field.

After working for an oil company for a while, which she found boring, and considering a job excavating dinosaurs, which she also had little interest in, she eventually made her way to New York, where she interviewed for a position at Columbia University. The manager wasn't really sure what to do with Tharp, and he finally asked her, "Can you draft?" Working on her drafting skills back at the university had finally paid off. Tharp got the job.

In 1948, Tharp began to work for a man named Bruce Heezen, who was managing a project to map the ocean floor. For a long time, people believed the ocean floor was just a flat surface covered by water. But when scientists began studying ocean depths, they quickly realized the ocean floor was anything but flat and simple. The ocean floor had canyons, ridges, mountains, and other features, just like on land. People had plenty of maps showing the topography of land, but nobody had a map of the ocean floor.

The invention of sonar made mapping the ocean floor possible. With sonar, it's possible to measure the depth of water. An instrument on board a ship sends a sound into the water. The sound echoes back to the ship after bouncing back from the ocean floor. A sonar system detects how long it takes the sound to return to the ship. This information is then used to calculate how deep the ocean is at that precise spot. The longer it takes a sound to echo back to the ship, the deeper the ocean.

Heezen went out to sea to collect sonar details, but Tharp had to stay back at the office. Women weren't allowed on research ships because they were considered bad luck at sea. Heezen sent all the data he collected back to Tharp. She converted the data into a detailed map of the ocean floor. This was before computers, so she did all her work by hand with only pens and rulers. Those drafting skills proved useful, allowing Tharp to draw the first 3D map of the ocean floor. This was a very challenging and detailed process because there was so much data for her to analyze. The ocean was massive.

WOMEN WEREN'T ALLOWED ON RESEARCH SHIPS BECAUSE THEY WERE CONSIDERED BAD LUCK AT SEA.

But as Tharp's maps began to take shape, she spotted something rather curious—a deep rift running down the middle of the Atlantic Ocean, surrounded by mountain ranges on both sides. This appeared like a V-shaped gap running right through the center of the mountains. Tharp checked and rechecked her numbers, but the data was solid. This wasn't merely a deep crack in the ocean floor; this was something more. This was a place where two masses of land had separated.

Tharp shared her findings with her boss. Heezen immediately rejected Tharp's maps, calling them "girl talk." What Tharp was reporting was not possible. Convinced she must have made a mistake, Heezen ordered Tharp to start all over again and redo the maps.

Heezen had good reason to dismiss Tharp's suggestion that a rift passed through the length of the Atlantic Ocean. If this were true, it would offer proof for an idea that was extremely unpopular at the time. If Heezen were to support this idea, he would be the laughingstock of the scientific community and bring shame on his lab and employer. This controversial theory was called continental drift. The theory suggested that at one time, all the continents of Earth were once combined, and that the continents had been slowly drifting apart for ages. This was a radical theory, especially because, if it were true, it would mean the continents were still drifting apart to this day. There was some scientific evidence to support this theory. For one thing, by looking at a map, one could see how the continents might fit together like the pieces of a jigsaw puzzle. Also, scientists had unearthed similar fossils in extremely different parts of the world. How could the same fossils be found in Africa and South America, separated by a wide ocean? Despite some supporting evidence, the theory of continental drift was widely considered in the scientific community to be a joke. There was no conceivable way to explain, through science, that the continents were drifting slowly apart.

Tharp did as she was asked. She went back and redid the maps. And her results were the same. A rift did, indeed, exist down the entire span of the Atlantic Ocean. This rift was caused as hot magma from deep inside the earth surfaced and cooled, causing the land to move apart. Here was evidence of plate tectonics, the idea that the surface of the earth is made up of plates that are constantly shifting and moving.

Tharp's maps proved that continental drift was real. Heezen published the data supporting plate tectonics and continental drift. Tharp's name was not included on any of the papers.

And yet, despite all of Tharp's evidence, the scientific community was still not convinced that continental drift was possible. One of the doubters was renowned ocean explorer Jacques Cousteau. He set out to disprove this theory once and for all. Cousteau attached a movie camera to a sled and towed it across the sea as his ship sailed across the ocean. What he saw shocked him. As his ship approached the mountain range known as the Mid-Atlantic Ridge, the camera captured footage of a very deep rift, splitting the mountain range in half, in the exact spot Tharp said it would be. Cousteau was so astonished he turned the ship around to film again. The footage was exactly the same. Tharp's maps were correct. There was, indeed, a deep rift in the Atlantic Ocean. Continental drift was real.

Tharp produced the first maps of the ocean floor, providing valuable insight to help oceanographers and geologists for years to come. This by itself was a remarkable accomplishment. But finding the rift valley was extraordinary. Tharp showed that the rift valley went all the way around the world for 40,000 miles. There is nothing bigger than that on planet Earth, and it was completely hidden until Tharp's discovery. And yet, Tharp's work has gone largely unnoticed, with Heezen taking most of the glory for the discovery. Tharp's contributions have only recently begun to be recognized. In 1997, she was honored by the Library of Congress as one of the four greatest cartographers of the twentieth century. They also included one of her maps in an exhibit where it hung alongside a rough draft of the Declaration of Independence. When Marie Tharp visited the exhibit and saw her map displayed and honored, she started to cry from joy. Finally, her work was considered more than just "girl talk."

What's the SCIENCE?

TODAY, EVERYONE KNOWS THAT Earth has seven continents. But that wasn't always the case. Millions of years ago, land on Earth looked nothing like the seven continents we know today. All the land on Earth was one giant continent. The supercontinent was called Pangaea. Imagine! You could drive a car from North America to Asia and never hit water—except cars wouldn't be invented for two hundred million years, but that's beside the point.

If you look carefully at a map, you will see proof that Pangaea existed. Looking at the shape of the continents, you might notice that they all fit together like puzzle pieces. Geologists who study the formation of the earth have collected other evidence in support of Pangaea. For example, matching dinosaur fossils have been found on the east coast of South America and the west coast of Africa. Today, there is a wide ocean between these coasts. The only explanation for these matching fossils is that at some time, these land masses were connected.

It turns out the earth's continents are always moving, even now. This is called continental drift. The movement is very slow, so you can't feel it, but it's there. In a million years, land on Earth will look very different from the maps of today.

Continental drift is caused by plate tectonics, which is the motion of large "plates" that move across the earth. The theory states that Earth's outer shell isn't actually stationary. The shell is broken up into several plates that slide across the earth. Each of these plates are different in size and shape. The plates move because of different forces from deep inside our planet.

Two plates that interact with each other will result in a geology

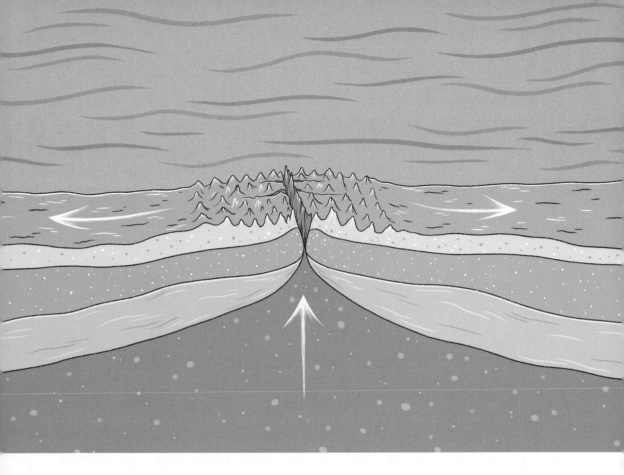

event. For instance, where two plates push together, the force of the interaction can cause the formation of mountains and volcanoes. It can also cause earthquakes. Sometimes two plates are pushed apart. This will cause a rift in the land.

The Mid-Atlantic Ridge is the border between several plates that are pulling away from each other. Since this is happening underwater, it creates a ridge and causes the ocean floor to spread.

ROSALIND FRANKLIN

1920-1958

Have you ever wondered why some people have brown hair and others red hair? Why some people are tall and others short? Why some people are right-handed and others left-handed? All these instructions come from something inside you called DNA. DNA stands for "deoxyribonucleic acid." It is one of the most important molecules in our bodies. DNA makes you who you are. It acts like a blueprint or recipe, telling your body what you're supposed to look like and how to function. Nobody has the same DNA as you.

For a long time, scientists had absolutely no idea how DNA worked. They wondered how DNA could transmit information to the body to allow it to function. Many scientists guessed that the *shape* of DNA was important to this process. If scientists could figure out how DNA was structured, they'd have a much better idea of how it worked.

From a very early age, Rosalind Franklin showed a brilliant mind. She did math problems for fun, and, like any good scientist, asked lots of questions. When her parents taught her about God, she asked, "How do you know He isn't a She?"

After World War II, Franklin's career as a scientist took her to prestigious King's College in London, England. The scientists working there had already started making some very interesting observations about the structure of DNA, and with Franklin's experience with X-ray technologies, she hoped that together as a team they could solve the DNA puzzle.

But working at King's College wasn't the dream job Rosalind Franklin had hoped it would be. Her male colleagues didn't welcome her onto the team. In those days, women scientists were considered unusual, and were often treated unfairly. For example, only men were allowed in the main common room where scientists had lunch, drank coffee, and shared ideas. Since Rosalind Franklin wasn't permitted to sit with her male colleagues, she missed out on a lot of collaboration.

SINCE ROSALIND FRANKLIN WASN'T PERMITTED TO SIT WITH HER MALE COLLEAGUES, SHE MISSED OUT ON A LOT OF COLLABORATION.

It was hardly a team effort.

To make matters worse, she did not get along with the partner she was assigned to work with. That partner's name was Maurice Wilkins. When Wilkins was told that he would be partnered with Franklin, he assumed she would be working as his assistant. He didn't take well to the idea that a woman would be his peer.

Franklin and Wilkins just couldn't get along in the lab. Pretty soon, the two of them stopped collaborating altogether on trying to decode the mysteries of DNA's structure. Wilkins quietly did his own work while, nearby, Franklin continued with her own research.

And waltzing right into the middle of these two feuding scientists came two other scientists: James Watson and Francis Crick.

It was easy for Franklin's partner, Wilkins, to follow along with Watson and Crick. He didn't much like Franklin, and finally he had another set of colleagues he could collaborate with and call his friends. To him, these were fine, scholarly men, and a much welcome improvement over his female partner. It didn't take a lot to convince Wilkins to turn his back on Franklin. It didn't even matter when Watson was horribly rude to Franklin. Shortly after

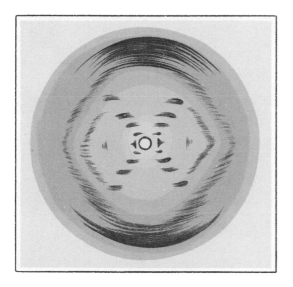

meeting her, Watson made this comment: "I wondered how she would look if she took off her glasses and did something novel with her hair."

And then Wilkins did the unthinkable. Without Rosalind Franklin's knowledge, he secretly gave Watson and Crick a very important piece of Franklin's research, known as "Photo 51." This picture, an X-ray image captured by Franklin, showed the structure of DNA. They called this structure the double helix. With the discovery of the double helix structure of DNA, our understanding of life was changed forever.

It was this Photo 51, shared with Watson and Crick without Franklin's permission, that led Watson, Crick, and Wilkins to be awarded with the Nobel Prize for *their* discovery of the structure of DNA. Rosalind Franklin's contribution was ignored.

As if it wasn't bad enough that the three men stole Franklin's research, years later, Watson had the nerve to personally attack Franklin in his book, *The Double Helix*. There, he characterized Franklin as unable to understand her own research. He said she was ugly, insulted her fashion, and called her some pretty bad names. Even his Noble Prize–winning buddies, Crick and Wilkins, begged Watson to take those parts out of his book, but he refused.

Rosalind Franklin died of cancer in 1958, four years before Watson, Crick, and Wilkins were awarded the Nobel Prize. She did not live long enough to see her colleagues steal the credit for her hard work. The good news is the world is beginning to accept the truth about Rosalind Franklin. Today, the scientific community is finally acknowledging that it was Rosalind Franklin's research that led to the discovery of DNA's structure. King's College, where Franklin did her DNA research, honored her in 2000 by renaming one of their buildings as the Franklin-Wilkins Building.

DNA WAS ONE OF science's most important breakthroughs. But how exactly does DNA work? It uses a special alphabet, made up of only four letters, which gives your body instructions on how it's supposed to look and how it's supposed to operate. These letters, also known as bases, are *A*, *T*, *C*, and *G*. The letters represent words: *A* = *adenine*, *T* = *thymine*, *C* = *cytosine*, and *G* = *guanine*.

Each of the bases in the DNA alphabet hates being alone, so it must always pair up with a friend. But these letters are like jigsaw-puzzle pieces. You can't force puzzle pieces to fit together in the wrong place! It's the same thing with the bases of the DNA alphabet. *A* and *T* fit together, and *C* and *G* fit together, but it's not possible for any other combinations to fit together. You'll never find, for example, *A* and *G* hanging out with each other.

These four letters—*A*, *T*, *C*, and *G*—make up every living creature on this planet. How can just four letters make up not only billions of unique humans, but also every single living animal and plant on Earth?

It's the *order* of the letters that is important. Humans have over three billion base pairs that can be arranged in so many ways. The order of everyone's DNA alphabet is slightly different, which makes everyone unique. Let's take a closer look at the structure of DNA.

We already know that *A* and *T* are always bonded, and *C* and *G* are always bonded.

To help hold together the base pairs, there is a supporting backbone on both sides of the DNA structure.

The structure looks a bit like a ladder, where the base pairs represent the rungs of the ladder. Except, DNA is a little more complicated than just a straight ladder. DNA is *twisted* to form what scientists call a double helix.

It was the discovery of this double helix structure of DNA that revolutionized the world of science and medicine forever. Most scientists agree that discovering the double helix structure of DNA was one of the most significant scientific achievements in the last century. Research into DNA has led to breakthrough medical discoveries. Doctors can now diagnose diseases earlier and more accurately. The discovery of DNA also led to new treatments for patients with conditions that were previously considered incurable.

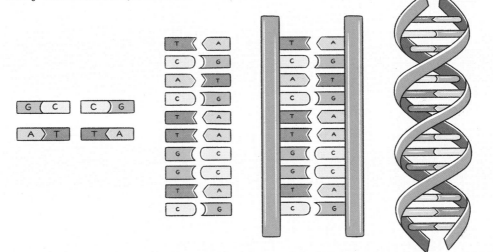

But the discovery of DNA impacted so much more than medicine. DNA from crime scenes has been used to prove that suspects were involved in crimes or to free people who were wrongly convicted. DNA research has also been very important for agriculture because it has allowed animal breeders to make stronger, more disease-resistant animals. It has also allowed farmers to produce more nutritious and hearty fruits and vegetables.

SOURCES

MARY ANNING

Montanari, Shaena. "Mary Anning: From Selling Seashells to One of History's Most Important Paleontologists." *Forbes*, May 21, 2015. https://www.forbes.com/sites/shaenamontanari/2015/05/21/mary-anning-from-selling-seashells-to-one-of-historys-most-important-paleontologists/?sh=6519c7f57ab3.

Pierce, Patricia. *Jurassic Mary: Mary Anning and the Primeval Monsters.* Stroud, Gloucestershire: The History Press, 2014.

Swaby, Rachel. *Headstrong: 52 Women Who Changed Science—and the World.* New York: Broadway Books, 2015.

Winick, Stephen. "She Sells Seashells and Mary Anning: Metafolklore with a Twist." *Folklife Today* (blog). Library of Congress, July 26, 2017. https://blogs.loc.gov/folklife/2017/07/she-sells-seashells-and-mary-anning-metafolklore-with-a-twist/.

JO ANDERSON

McCormick, Cyrus. *The Century of the Reaper.* Boston and New York: Houghton Mifflin Company, 1931.

McCormick Reaper Centennial Source Material. Madison: Wisconsin Historical Society, 1954.

McNamara, Robert. "Invention of the McCormick Reaper." *ThoughtCo*, June 21, 2019. https://www.thoughtco.com/mccormick-reaper-1773393.

Memorial of Robert McCormick, Being a Brief History of His Life, Character, and Inventions, Including the Early History of the McCormick Reaper. Chicago: Barnard & Gunthorp, 1885.

Rhodes, Karl. "Reaping the Benefits of the Reaper." *Econ Focus*, third/fourth quarter, 2016. https://www.richmondfed.org/-/media/richmondfedorg/publications/research/econ_focus/2016/q3-4/economic_history.pdf.

ANTONIO MEUCCI

Bellis, Mary. "Antonio Meucci: Did Meucci Invent the Telephone Before Alexander

Graham Bell?" *ThoughtCo*, July 3, 2019. https://www.thoughtco.com/antonio -meucci-4071768.

Chaparro, Laura. "Antonio Meucci, the Italian Immigrant Who Couldn't Patent the Telephone." *OpenMind*, October 18, 2017. https://www.bbvaopenmind.com/en /science/leading-figures/antonio-meucci-the-italian-immigrant-who-couldnt-patent -the-telephone/.

"Congressional Record: Tribute to Mr. Antonio Meucci," Digital Public Library of America, http://dp.la/item/c50ba03fa776ec4f9ae34ce3285912ee.

"Meucci's Claims to the Telephone—With Description of His Instrument and 10 Figures." *Scientific American Supplement* XX, no. 520 (December 19, 1885).

BENJAMIN BRADLEY

American Colonization Society. "Intelligence: Another Slave Freed." *The African Repository* XXXV, no. 12 (December 1859).

Gordon, Jacob U., *The Black Male in White America*. Hauppauge, NY: Nova Science Publishers, January 1, 2003.

Haskins, Jim. *Outward Dreams: Black Inventors and Their Inventions*. New York: Walker & Company, September 1, 2003.

"Purchase of the Freedom of a Maryland Slave." *The National Era*, October 27, 1859. https://www.loc.gov/resource/sn84026752/1859-10-27/ed-1/?q=%22benjamin +bradley%22&sp=1&r=-1.216,-0.114,3.433,1.434,0.

Spangenburg, Ray, Kit Moser, and Steven Otfinoski. *African Americans in Science, Math, and Invention (A to Z of African Americans)*. rev. ed. New York: Facts on File, 2011.

CARLOS JUAN FINLAY

Hill, Martin. "Walter Reed and the Yellow Fever Experiments." *Decoded Past*, May 26, 2013. https://decodedpast.com/walter-reed-and-the-yellow-fever-experiments/.

Liebowitz, Daniel. "Carlos Finlay, Walter Reed, and the Politics of Imperialism in Early Tropical Medicine." *The Pharos* 75, no. 1 (June 2012).

Orenstein, Alexander J. "Memorial Address—Carlos Juan Finlay, Class of 1855 and Back Pages." *Yellow Fever, a Symposium in Commemoration of Carlos Juan Finlay*, 1955. Paper 1. https://jdc.jefferson.edu/yellow_fever_symposium/1.

Taylor, Milton W. *Viruses and Man: A History of Interactions*. New York: Springer, 2014.

Warmflash, David. "Carlos J. Finlay." *Visionlearning* SCIRE-2, no. 1 (2015). https://www .visionlearning.com/en/library/Inside-Science/58/Carlos-J.-Finlay/217.

ANNA WESSELS WILLIAMS

Bailey, Brooke. *The Remarkable Lives of 100 Women Healers and Scientists*. Avon, MA: Adams Media Corporation, 1994.

SOURCES

Chung, King-Thom. *Women Pioneers of Medical Research: Biographies of 25 Outstanding Scientists.* Jefferson, NC: McFarland & Company, 2009.

Emrich, John S. "Anna Wessels Williams, M.D.: Infectious Disease Pioneer and Public Health Advocate." *AAI Newsletter* (March/April 2012). https://www.aai.org/AAISite /media/About/History/Articles/AAI_History_004.pdf.

Swaby, Rachel. *Headstrong: 52 Women Who Changed Science—and the World.* New York: Broadway Books, 2015.

Yount, Lisa. *A to Z of Women in Science and Math.* New York: Facts on File, 1999.

NETTIE STEVENS

Brush, Stephen G. "Nettie M. Stevens and the Discovery of Sex Determination by Chromosomes." *Isis* 69, no. 2 (1978): 163–172. https://www.jstor.org/stable/230427.

Cox, Troy. "Studies in Spermatogenesis (1905), by Nettie Maria Stevens." *Embryo Project Encyclopedia*, January 22, 2014. http://embryo.asu.edu/handle/10776/7511.

Gelling, Cristy. "Nettie Stevens: Sex Chromosomes and Sexism." *Genes to Genomes*, March 31, 2016. https://genestogenomes.org/nettie-stevens-sex-chromosomes-and -sexism/.

Morgan, T. H. "The Scientific Work of Miss N. M. Stevens." *Science* 36, no. 928 (1912): 468–470. https://www.jstor.org/stable/1636618.

Resnick, Brian. "Nettie Stevens Discovered XY Sex Chromosomes. She Didn't Get Credit Because She Had Two X's." *Vox*, July 7, 2017. https://www.vox.com/2016 /7/7/12105830/nettie-stevens-genetics-gender-sex-chromosomes.

Swaby, Rachel. *Headstrong: 52 Women Who Changed Science—and the World.* New York: Broadway Books, 2015.

LISE MEITNER

American Physical Society. "This Month in Physics History; December 1938: Discovery of Nuclear Fission." *APS NEWS* 16, no. 11 (December 2007). https:// www.aps.org/publications/apsnews/200712/physicshistory.cfm?pagesfor_linkbar= /physicists/index.cfm.

Bradford, Alina. "Lise Meitner: Life, Findings and Legacy." *Live Science*, March 29, 2018. https://www.livescience.com/62162-lise-meitner-biography.html.

Fine, Melanie. "The Abduction of Lise Meitner." *Huffpost.* March 27, 2017. https:// www.huffpost.com/entry/the-abduction-of-lise-meitner_b_58d974cae4b0e6062d92 2ff1.

Hanly, Beverly. "Feb. 11, 1939: Lise Meitner, 'Our Madame Curie.'" *WIRED*, February 11, 2010. https://www.wired.com/2010/02/0211lise-meitner-publishes-nuclear -fission/.

Knutsen, Elise. "This Brilliant Woman Pioneered Nuclear Technology, But Her Male

Colleague Got a Nobel Prize For It." *Medium*, August 2, 2017. https://medium
.com/s/the-matilda-effect/lise-meitner-matilda-effect-74c19c65d944.

Sime, Ruth Lewin. *Lise Meitner: A Life in Physics*. Berkeley: University of California
Press, 1997.

Swaby, Rachel. *Headstrong: 52 Women Who Changed Science—and the World*. New York:
Broadway Books, 2015.

ALICE BALL

Brewster, Carisa D. "How the Woman Who Found a Leprosy Treatment Was Almost
Lost to History." *National Geographic*, February 28, 2018. https://www.national
geographic.com/news/2018/02/alice-ball-leprosy-hansens-disease-hawaii-womens
-history-science/.

Swaby, Rachel. *Headstrong: 52 Women Who Changed Science—and the World*. New York:
Broadway Books, 2015.

HILDE MANGOLD

Doty, Maria. "Hilde Mangold (1898–1924)." *Embryo Project Encyclopedia*, May 9, 2011.
https://embryo.asu.edu/handle/10776/1743.

Elliott, Ellen. "Women In Science: Hilde Mangold and the Embryonic Organizer." *The
Jackson Laboratory Jax Blog*, October 20, 2016. https://www.jax.org/news-and-insights
/jax-blog/2016/october/women-in-science-hilde-mangold#.

Magner, Lois N. *A History of Life Sciences*. Boca Raton, FL: CRC Press, 2002.

Riley, Alex. "How Your Embryo Knew What To Do." *Nautilus*, November 26, 2015.
https://nautil.us/issue/30/identity/how-your-embryo-knew-what-to-do.

Swaby, Rachel. *Headstrong: 52 Women Who Changed Science—and the World*. New York:
Broadway Books, 2015.

CHIEN-SHIUNG WU

Ouellette, Jennifer. "Madame Wu and the Holiday Experiment That Changed Physics
Forever." *Gizmodo*, December 31, 2015. https://gizmodo.com/madame-wu-and-the
-holiday-experiment-that-changed-physi-1749319896.

Scutts, Joanna. "The Manhattan Project Physicist Who Fought for Equal Rights for
Women." *Time*, June 14, 2016. https://time.com/4366137/chien-shiung-wu-history/.

Swaby, Rachel. *Headstrong: 52 Women Who Changed Science—and the World*. New York:
Broadway Books, 2015.

Weinstock, Maia. "Channeling Ada Lovelace: Chien-Shiung Wu, Courageous Hero of
Physics." *Scientific American*, October 15, 2013. https://blogs.scientificamerican.com
/guest-blog/channeling-ada-lovelace-chien-shiung-wu-courageous-hero-of-physics/.

SOURCES

MARIE THARP

Blakemore, Erin. "Seeing Is Believing: How Marie Tharp Changed Geology Forever." *Smithsonian Magazine*, August 30, 2016. https://www.smithsonianmag.com/history /seeing-believing-how-marie-tharp-changed-geology-forever-180960192/.

Debakcsy, Dale. "Making Continents Move: The Ocean Cartography of Marie Tharp." *Women You Should Know*, February 22, 2018. https://womenyoushouldknow.net /cartography-marie-tharp/.

Felt, Hali. *Soundings: The Story of the Remarkable Woman Who Mapped the Ocean Floor.* New York: Henry Holt and Company, 2012.

Swaby, Rachel. *Headstrong: 52 Women Who Changed Science—and the World*. New York: Broadway Books, 2015.

Washburn, Michael. "Floating Ideas." *New York Times*, January 25, 2013. https://www .nytimes.com/2013/01/27/books/review/soundings-about-marie-tharp-by-hali-felt .html.

ROSALIND FRANKLIN

Lloyd, Robin. "Rosalind Franklin and DNA: How Wronged Was She?" *Scientific American*, November 3, 2010. https://blogs.scientificamerican.com/observations /rosalind-franklin-and-dna-how-wronged-was-she/.

Maddox, Brenda. *Rosalind Franklin: The Dark Lady of DNA*. New York: HarperCollins, 2002.

Swaby, Rachel. *Headstrong: 52 Women Who Changed Science—and the World*. New York: Broadway Books, 2015.

In April 2019, two remarkable images made the news, becoming instantly famous.

The first image was that of a black hole. With black holes, the force of gravity is so strong that anything that comes near it is swallowed up. Nothing can escape the forces of a black hole, not even light. Scientists had known for a long time that black holes existed in theory, but they were never able to see a black hole.

Until that moment in April 2019.

For the first time, the world was able to see an actual picture of a black hole. The picture showed a dark shadow surrounded by a fiery ring. Scientists were able to create this picture by piecing together many images taken by telescopes from around the world. Now we were able to see what was once believed to be unseeable, an image of a real black hole.

The second remarkable image was that of Dr. Katie Bouman.

Dr. Bouman was the twenty-nine-year-old postgraduate student who made the black hole image possible. She developed the computer program that pieced together images and data from telescopes around the world. Her program was responsible for assembling all the data and constructing the image of the black hole that was, eventually, broadcasted around the world.

Dr. Bouman sat in front of her computer screen, watching the image of the black hole begin to take form as her computer program compiled the data.

And when the program had finished running and the black hole appeared on Dr. Bouman's screen, someone snapped a photograph of her reaction.

It was the face of wonder. She had her hands clasped over her mouth, a giddy grin peeking out beyond her fingers. Her eyes were wide in amazement. Behind her was the image that had formed on her screen of the black hole. It was a moment of triumph. Years and years of hard work had finally paid off. Dr. Bouman was looking at the first ever picture of a black hole on her computer screen.

The photo of Dr. Bouman went viral. It was shared across Twitter, Instagram, and Facebook millions of times. People celebrated the young woman scientist who gave us the spectacular image that was once thought to be impossible. Since it was her smiling picture that was shared around the world, she quickly became the face of the black hole discovery. Dr. Bouman became a role model for young girls and proved that smart women deserved to be a part of science.

But just as quickly as Dr. Bouman was celebrated, a different story began to emerge. This story was started by internet trolls. An internet troll is basically an internet bully. They try to post messages online to intentionally upset or provoke a reaction. Many times what trolls post is wrong or grossly overexaggerated.

Within a few hours of Dr. Bouman's picture going viral, the internet trolls went to work, declaring that she did not deserve the credit for the black hole discovery. They started spreading misinformation that Bouman didn't actually write the majority of the computer program responsible for the black hole image. These trolls were trying to convince people that Bouman didn't deserve the accolades for the discovery, but instead her male colleague Andrew Chael deserved all the credit. They said that Chael had written most of the code for the project, not Bouman.

AUTHOR'S NOTE

Dr. Bouman's entire reputation and years of groundbreaking work were being challenged publicly. The internet trolls said horrible and demeaning things about her. They called her a fraud. And worse. The assaults were so troubling that she had to turn off her phone and social media.

It is true that the image of the black hole cannot be credited to just one person, as is often the case with scientific discoveries. There were over two hundred people involved in the black hole project. And Dr. Bouman was quick to point out that she was by no means solely responsible for the discovery. She acknowledged that a team of scientists from around the world collaborated together to make the image possible.

But Andrew Chael, Dr. Bouman's male colleague who the internet trolls claimed was the real developer of the program, publicly defended her. He said none of the trolls' claims were true. He acknowledged that Dr. Bouman's contributions to the program were genuine and slammed the trolls for trying to diminish her hard work.

But why were the internet trolls so quick to attack Dr. Bouman and challenge her part in the project?

It's a familiar story.

For hundreds of years, powerful forces have worked to take away hard-earned credit from women, people of color, immigrants, and other marginalized groups. And it's still happening today.

It was difficult enough for Dr. Bouman to gain success in a male-dominated field. But then to be leveled with baseless attacks must have been crushing.

I chose to write *Stolen Science* not as a cautionary tale for readers. I chose to write this book to show that despite obstacles, scientists of all races, colors, and religions have gone on to perform groundbreaking science. While their names may not be well known, their contributions have been revolutionary.

AUTHOR'S NOTE

When I started engineering school at Columbia University, my freshman class was only 17 percent women. I recall going to a professor's office hours for extra help in a very challenging physics course. Instead of answering my questions, the professor said to me, "Maybe you're not cut out for this class." I left his office in tears. I reflect back on that moment often. The whole point of holding office hours for extra help is to . . . let your students ask for help, which is what I did. I was being a responsible student, taking the extra initiative to be successful in the course. Did I deserve that response from the teacher? Of course not. Did my male classmates get the same response from the teacher? No. As a female student in the engineering school, I had to work harder than my male classmates to prove I belonged. And that's not fair.

Luckily, my alma mater, Columbia University, has made great improvements since my time there. The engineering school is now nearly 50 percent women and has leveled the available opportunities for women in the program. This is, indeed, encouraging. But as we can see from the story of Dr. Katie Bouman, women still have a way to go to be fully embraced in the science and engineering community.

ACKNOWLEDGMENTS

Writing a book may be solitary, but publishing a book is the work of many, in great and small ways. I am grateful to so many who have been with me on this journey.

A huge thank-you to my agent, Clelia Gore, and the team at Martin Literary Management. Clelia has been my champion since the day I met her. She has turned me from an aspiring writer to a published author and has been a true partner in this journey. I can't thank her enough for believing in me and for encouraging me to write the books we both believe in. Thank you, my friend.

Thank you to the team at Bloomsbury, and especially the brilliant editor Susan Dobinick. From day one, you believed in this book and what it stood for. You knew *Stolen Science* was more than just a nonfiction reference book. Together we are inspiring the next generation of young scientists by bringing these important, forgotten stories to life.

A special thank-you to illustrator Gaby D'Alessandro. Most people who know me know I can barely draw a stick figure. Artwork isn't my area of strength. I'm so jealous of artists who can create beautiful images I barely have the ability to imagine in my head, let alone craft on a canvas. Gaby's stunning artwork made the story of these important scientists come to life beyond words, and she reminds us that art and science are always connected.

A huge thank-you to the Wisconsin Historical Society and the McCormick-

ACKNOWLEDGMENTS

International Harvester Collection for providing fantastic source material on Jo Anderson. Also, my gratitude goes to the librarians at the Library of Congress for assisting me with my research. They are truly special humans. If you're in Washington, DC, the Library of Congress is a magical place that you must visit.

To the chemical and industrial engineering departments at Columbia University, I am grateful for all the doors you opened for me. The engineering school taught me more than just thermodynamics, data structures, and circuits. It taught me to embrace my inner scientist, inspired me to keep learning even when I think I've learned enough, and to stand resolute as a confident professional. For my Columbia engineering friends who helped get me through nine a.m. Friday classes, eight-hour study sessions in Low Library, midterms, finals, and more—I could not have made it without you. Ziona and Bozena: there weren't many of us girls, but we were strong and mighty. Friends for life.

My gratitude to Carter Sargent for his sensitivity read and excellent suggestions.

For my writing friends, especially the #MGBetaReaders Melanie, Colten, Karen, Rhonda, Brian, Jean, Jeff, Brooks, KiWing, Ronni, Jo, Jessika, Dana, Akos, Laurie, Gail, Jen, Abby, Chris, and Gail: you help me find the strength and motivation to continue as a writer. Writing books alongside all of you is an honor.

Thank you to my parents, immigrants who came to this country looking for a better life for their children. I think it's safe to say my brothers and I have had a charmed life because of all your sacrifices. I was a young girl with a knack for math and science, but you never made me feel that a girl wasn't worthy of an education. On the contrary, you worked literally night and day and sacrificed much to give me the chance to succeed. And while my mom may complain that I never have the right outfits or matching accessories for my business meetings, I hope I've made my parents proud despite my lack of fashion sense—a scientist believes in sensible shoes over fashion any day!

Thank you to my husband, Jeff, for "helping me" with my college computer programming assignments. I'm an engineer because of you. You will always be more technical than me, and I'm good with that. Women in science thrive when they have the support of male colleagues and partners, and you have always been my biggest cheerleader and champion. When I'm stressed out juggling work, writing, the house, and the kids, I often reflect on the words of my hero and fellow Columbia grad, Ruth Bader Ginsburg: "Women can have everything, but not at the same time." Well, I feel I have had everything, but only because of you, Jeff. You've made all my dreams come true.

For my boys—Harrison, Sammy, and Nate—keep asking questions and searching for answers. Know there is always more to learn, and different ways of seeing the world. *Stolen Science* is about discovery and finding the truth. Always dig deep and look for the truth. This book is for you.